REAL LIFE
Marriage

AUTHOR OF *THOROUGHLY MARRIED*

LUCY & DENNIS GUERNSEY

REAL LIFE

Marriage

WORD BOOKS
PUBLISHER
WACO, TEXAS

A DIVISION OF
WORD, INCORPORATED

Library of Congress Cataloging-in-Publication Data:

Guernsey, Lucy, 1940–
  Real life marriage.
  1. Marriage—Religious aspects—Christianity.
  2. Guernsey, Lucy, 1940–   . 3. Guernsey, Dennis B.
  I. Guernsey, Dennis B. II. Title.
  BV835.G84 1987   248.8'4   87–25319
  ISBN 0-8499-3095-2

Printed in the United States of America

7 8 9 8 RRD 9 8 7 6 5 4 3 2 1

To the men and women who
through the years
as clients and friends have taught us
what real life is all about

Contents

Introduction

More than ten years have gone by since Dennis wrote *Thoroughly Married*. That book was about marital communication in general and sexual communication in particular. But of course, like any marriage book, it was also about our own marriage. And so Lucy stepped in as an active editor, as was chronicled in the preface.

A lot has changed over those ten years since *Thoroughly Married* appeared. Each of us has changed as an individual, and our marriage has undergone changes, too. In a sense, the way we have chosen to go about writing this sequel reflects those changes. For we are writing *Real Life Marriage* as full coauthors, with each of us contributing to, taking responsibility for, and receiving credit for the end product.

We have had to work hard on this joint effort, just as we have had to work at our marriage. And there have been struggles, just as there are in any real-life marriage. For instance, we have disagreed over just how much of our personal lives to share. Dennis always wants to share more, Lucy less. Each of us has tried to listen and to hear what the other is saying and to adjust our demands and expectations accordingly. The result, we hope, is a book that is honest and genuinely helpful while at the same time staying within the boundaries of good taste and appropriate self-disclosure.

What is before you, then, is in many ways a metaphor of our marriage as it is today. We can say with some degree of confidence that we have worked out our own partnership without any status differential as to who is "senior" and who is "junior." We have worked at learning how to "mutually submit" to one another. The natural wisdom of this world is that such equality can't work. But, as with the bumblebee, what shouldn't fly does.

Our commitment in this book is to bear witness to the grace of God. He has sustained our marriage through some rough times. At the same time, his grace has facilitated our individual development. Growing as persons and growing as partners are not necessarily mutually exclusive, but the process can be complex. The paradox is that what God alone can do still requires a lot of work on the part of the couple.

That brings us to another point, which has to do with the romantic expectations that seem to have emerged in Christian literature about what people can and should expect from marriage. We have come to the conclusion that for most people, the Christian *ideal* of marriage as it is presently held out is virtually unattainable. As our friend Diana Richman Garland of Southern Seminary has said, we have "upped the ante so high as to make the ideal beyond the reach of the vast majority of marriages."

We hope in this book to speak to this issue. In some ways we have deliberately tried to *lower* expectations from what is "ideal" to what is more nearly "real."

Chapter 1 of this book, then, addresses the "ideal-vs.-real" tension as it occurs in marriage. We look at five "styles" of long-term marriages and how each evolves—and what a couple can do if they would like to change their marriage style.

Chapters 2 and 3 contain our views on intimacy. Not everyone is capable of the same degree of intimacy. What often results is a terrifying bind and a frustrating lifestyle. In fact, we believe differences in intimacy needs have contributed to some of the general disillusionment over marriage in contemporary society.

Chapters 4 and 5 deal with what makes people distinct in terms of the way they perceive the world and how those perceptions shape communication between marriage partners. In many ways, what we have worked out in our own marriage stems in large measure from the understanding we have gained about how we are different from one another and what demands those differences make on our marriage.

What do you do when both partners in a marriage work outside the home? The term often used to describe such marriages is the "dual career" marriage. Chapter 6 has to do with the day-to-day problems and struggles that the majority of American marriages live with now that we have become a two-paycheck culture.

Chapters 7 and 8 take a look at the issue of values and how married couples can be caught in a web created by their differing value systems. At least some of the pain that is reflected in marriage can be traced back to the "ground" of values we have chosen to build our lives upon.

Finally, chapters 9 through 11 focus upon the parenting task, especially as it affects marriage. In this section we talk about marital changes over the family life cycle, what it means to do the best that you can do as a parent without expecting perfection, and how to face the very real issues of attachment, separation, loss, and grief both as a couple and as a family.

At the writing of this book, we have been married twenty-seven years. And we are still "thoroughly married," though there is a bit of the wizened veteran about both of us.

We hope our "war stories" will encourage most of you. That is our intent.

We are aware, however, that our story is in no way unique. There are many others who, given the chance, could tell their own special history and in so doing give witness to the marvelous God we serve and the grace he has shed upon us all. In this sense, our story is their story as well.

Altadena, California   DENNIS AND LUCY GUERNSEY
March 1987

Whatever Happened to the Wedding Pictures?

1985 was a significant year for us. We celebrated our twenty-fifth wedding anniversary, and we participated in the marriage of our eldest daughter. These two milestones of middle age occurred within three months of each other. We had now been married longer than we had been single. And we were now the parents of an emerging young woman who was beginning her own marriage journey, just as we had so long ago.

Our daughter's marriage in particular provoked a sense of déjà vu for us both. We couldn't help but remember when we had stood in a similar place twenty-five years earlier.

As is the case for most people, our wedding day was one of the most exciting days of our lives: "We're actually getting married!" After the craziness of the engagement, the headaches of planning the wedding, the doubts about whether or not we were doing the right thing, everything was in place and the day had finally arrived.

Many couples who look back on their wedding remember few of the details because the excitement and stress of the day produced a kind of emotional haze—almost like the self-protective state of shock the body goes into when it has been injured. Others look back on their wedding with a surrealistic vividness. They feel almost like passengers on an ocean liner ready to embark on a round-the-world cruise with bands playing, streamers flying, balloons rising. Every event of the day gives the experience a larger-than-life quality.

However the couple reacts, a wedding is a significant event. And to capture that significance, modern custom ordains that there be wedding pictures.

The bridal party stands elegantly at attention as the photographer attempts to capture the importance of the day. Never before and probably never again will the bride and groom look as charming and delightful as they do in these pictures. Mothers and fathers who have just become mothers-in-law and fathers-in-law stand dutifully still for the camera. Their fears, if any, are buried beneath the joy of the wedding.

The newlyweds pose excitedly—their happy expectations clearly on their faces: "We will be forever happy. We will be committed to one another. We will be devoted. We will meet each other's needs. Nothing and no one will ever come between us."

The wedding party looks on with benign approval. And it's all captured on film. The pictures will always be there to remind the couple of their promises.

One way to interpret the importance of the wedding pictures is to say that culturally they represent the wishes and expectations that the families and the community have for the new couple. The pictures also can be seen to represent the romantic idealism our culture has attached to marriage. When the two streams of community and culture merge, they influence the couple's own expectations of what their marriage promises to be.

The wedding day with its wedding pictures chronicles the beginning of a voyage colored by optimism, hope, and promise. The romantic idealism has been both institutionalized and internalized. The couple and their community both agree: this marriage will be special.

Welcome to the Real World!

Just how different will it really be? Virtually all couples soon come to realize that the reality of marriage is markedly different from the promise. Somewhere between five and ten years into the marriage, the two people who posed so tenderly for their wedding pictures look at each other across the breakfast table, and each sees someone far different from the person who stood next to him or her on their wedding day.

Both spouses have changed physically; the slim, trim, athletic body of the wedding day (and wedding night) has developed a paunch or stretch marks. And both have changed emotionally as well. The delightful "free spirit" now seems irresponsible; the logical, analytical mind inexpressive and lacking in warmth and empathy. The easygoing laid-back spirit has evolved into a terrible housekeeper, and the comfortably dependable soul has become boring and stuck in a rut. Over time, those qualities that once attracted us grate on our nerves.

Welcome to the real world of real marriage—when the day-to-day reality fails to live up to the ideal promise of the wedding pictures.

And so now comes the decision: *Which do you keep, the pictures or the person?*

The solution for more and more people in the latter half of the twentieth century is to throw away the person and keep the pictures. This process is called divorce. But what about the others, those who choose not to divorce? What can be said of them? Why do they stay together? What kind of marriage can they have?

Five Kinds of Lasting Marriage

One way we have come to answer these questions is to think in terms of five kinds of long-lasting marriages as identified in a research study done by J. L. Cuber and Peggy Haroff at the University of California at Berkeley in the mid-1960s. Even though the research is more than twenty years old, Cuber and Haroff's insights still provide useful pegs on which to hang our thinking.

These five types of marriages represent *intact, enduring* relationships. But that doesn't mean all five types are positive. In fact, the first two types of marriages described by Cuber and Haroff can be thought of as negative and destructive. We mention them here primarily to point out that not everybody who stays married does so for healthy reasons. But we hope also to show that even those in destructive marriages can change the way they relate to one another.

The first kind of marriage in Cuber and Haroff's model is the *conflict-habituated* marriage. Such marriages are marked by constant and recurring hassles and arguments—sometimes even violence. The reasons these people fuss and fight so much of the time vary according to the personalities and cultures involved. Sometimes the conflict is due in part to substance abuse, destructive and neurotic needs, or badly ingrained habits. Some people just like to fight. But research studies indicate that most of these marriages are marked by personal and relational pain, even though the couple chooses not to divorce.

The second kind of marriage is the *devitalized* marriage. It is a marriage in which the partners are living in an empty shell with, perhaps, the memory of what used to be a "good" marriage. A devitalized marriage is one in which the flame of the relationship has gone out, but the couple stays committed—not to one another, but to the institution. For the most part, they live separate lives, yet they maintain the appearance of being married.

The next three types of marriage as identified by Cuber and Haroff can be thought of as being more positive and

16

constructive than either the conflict-habituated or the devital-ized relationships.

The third type is the *passive-congenial* marriage. In a passive-congenial marriage, the partners live parallel lives, but not in the empty-shell manner of the devitalized marriage. The partners are usually friends, but not necessarily best friends. They get along and have worked out a relationship in which there is typically more separateness than there is togetherness. The marriage is characterized by a quality of stability. At times it is difficult for the passive-congenial couple to understand why other marriages experience conflict or require such work. Often, as far as they are concerned, being married just "happens."

Still another type of marriage identified by Cuber and Haroff is the *vital* marriage. This kind of relationship is typically marked by frequent interaction and communication, interspersed with times of separateness. In a vital marriage, the married partners experience times of intimacy, but not at the expense of the identities of the individuals. In many ways, the vital marriage best typifies the "ideal" marriage of the 1980s. The couple often thinks of themselves as best friends.

The fifth and last type of marriage identified in the research is the *total* marriage. In a total marriage, the partners' lives are so intermixed and interwoven with one another that it is difficult for others to distinguish between the two. Often the couple share a career as well as a marriage. Their goals are virtually interchangeable. They live together, work together, play together, and love together. In terms of friendship, frequently they are one another's *only* close friend.

Which Works Best?

And so we have five kinds of enduring marriages—two normally thought of as being unhealthy and three usually considered healthy.

Contemporary wisdom suggests that the first two kinds

of marriages—the conflict-habituated and the devitalized—would be better off if they were allowed to die. In fact, our experience indicates those are the ones that *do* die. Many of the supposedly "good" marriages that we have seen end in divorce were perceived by one or both partners as either marked by steady and constant conflict or an emptiness that could no longer be endured.

But we would suggest that the contemporary wisdom about what kind of marriages should continue sometimes leads the couple to pull the plug prematurely, before the issues have been fully explored and all the options measured and evaluated. The key is not to quit simply and only because the marriage is not living up to the ideal. The key is learning to face reality and then working together to build a healthier marital style.

The ideal marriage is typically thought of as being somewhere between the last two types, the vital and the total. After all, aren't we taught that "the two shall become one flesh"? Anything less is often thought of as failure, or at least as less than God's will for marriage.

But our own personal experience is that during the history of our life together we have experienced *all five* types of marriages, each at different times of our life. That we would pass through all five types as if they were stages makes sense when you consider our individual backgrounds and family histories.

Dennis, for instance, was raised as the only child of a single mother. He remembers very little conflict at home, but also not a lot of closeness or togetherness. His relationship with his mother could be thought of as being passive-congenial.

In contrast, Lucy was raised as the eldest of six children. Her home was marked by constant interaction and communication. Something was always going on. In terms of the Cuber and Haroff types, Lucy's was a vital family.

In a very real sense, our family backgrounds established our expectations as to what our marriage would be like.

Dennis envisioned a kind of parallel peacefulness, while Lucy envisioned a kind of active vitality. And no less than two years into the marriage, while Dennis was attending seminary, our differing expectations began to clash. Lucy increasingly yearned for interaction and closeness, while Dennis opted for peace and distance.

Lucy's reaction to this conflict of expectations was to push and nag (after all, as the oldest of six brothers and sisters she was accustomed to taking charge). Unfortunately, Dennis's response to her pushing was to withdraw and move farther and farther away. And the more he withdrew, the more Lucy pushed. In the midst of seminary, while Dennis was busy studying the Bible and preparing for ministry in the church, our marriage became conflict-habituated. To one degree or another that pattern lasted for several years, although we kept it to ourselves.

Then approximately seven years into our marriage, Lucy grew tired. She decided that she had had enough and she stopped trying to make the marriage work. Dennis was preoccupied with his work and not working all that hard at the relationship, either. And so the marriage drifted into a pattern of devitalization.

It was a terrifying time for us. Fortunately, by God's grace, we caught ourselves before it was too late. But the basic problem was still there; we had mutually exclusive expectations.

Our solution was to try to figure out how to build a marriage that had enough distance for Dennis yet enough closeness for Lucy. But this meant Lucy had to lower her expectations and Dennis had to work harder. Clearly we weren't going to have the ideal marriage promised by our wedding pictures. Like all married couples, we eventually had to face real life as real people.

As we said, at some time or another our marriage has seemed to fit each of Cuber and Haroff's patterns. This may be true for some of you. Or even if you haven't experienced all of the types, you may have experienced one or more of them, perhaps even simultaneously.

At a recent couples conference we led, a woman came up to us at the end of the presentation in which we discussed the reality of marriage as reflected in Cuber and Haroff's five types. She was terribly upset and agitated because she had found herself to be in all of the categories all at once, depend-ing on which day of the week or what time of the year it was.

Our answer was that that's the way it is with "types." They're not precise; they're only useful. But they can help us identify where we might be at any given time and where we'd like to be heading.

Changing Your Marriage Style

So, what if you find yourself in one type of marriage and would like to change? Suppose, for example, you find your marriage to be like one of the two "destructive" types. What can you do? Several suggestions based on our own experience may be helpful.

First of all, you have to face facts—to "own" the reality of the situation. This is what happened to us when our marriage reached its time of devitalization. Before we could change, both of us had to face where we were in our relationship.

We also had to acknowledge that both our perceptions of reality were valid and equally "real." The tendency during dif-ficult times is to blame the other person in the relationship and to become defensive. But neither of these responses is helpful. Even if your viewpoints are totally different, the truth for your marriage is that both perceptions are real—in the same way that one coin can have two sides yet still be the same coin.

The next step in the process is to determine what your expectations are. Where do you each want to go? And how do your expectations compare with reality? Expectations lie in-side us like unused blueprints; until they are made explicit, they can't be dealt with. In our own marriage, until we under-stood and faced the differences between us in terms of our needs for closeness and distance, we weren't able to come to any agreement regarding the direction we wanted the marriage to go.

It was at this point in our relationship that we came face to face with our own conflict between the ideal and the real in marriage. And we believe this is the point where real growth in marriage begins.

We had to face that fact in our own marriage. Each of us was trying to meet our own internalized ideal in our own way, but our ideals were different and, in a sense, mutually exclusive. We realized we had to find a way to compromise. You can imagine the amount of work it has taken over the years.

This brings us to our last suggestion: the work never ceases. At least it hasn't for us. It just seems to be a part of being human, living life in the arena of reality rather than the arena of idealism. If things are going to change, we must face the facts and decide to do the work that is necessary to make the change happen. Often the work is harder than it appears on the surface. Fortunately, in our case the work has become a part of our life together and even contributes to the satisfaction of being married. Besides, the work has made our play possible—and we definitely like the play!

Facing Up to Reality

What we are trying to say is that real marriage for real people involves an accommodation with reality based upon the personalities, backgrounds, and abilities of those who are in it. A decision to keep any romantic ideal alive in face of an inability to deliver the goods results only in frustration. For some, that frustration leads to divorce. For others who choose not to actually divorce, the decision to cling desperately to the ideal leads to an emptiness of lives together marked more by habit than by relationship.

So what does the Christian church have to say to this situation? For the most part, in our opinion, not much that is different or helpful. When Christians experience marital difficulties and turn to the hundreds of books and films generated by the Christian community, they usually find volumes which merely reinforce the romantic ideals of society at large—or which add still another set of even higher ideals designed just for Christian couples.

The purpose of most of this literature is to inspire Christian couples to strive for better marriages. But what more often transpires is a collision between the continued call for perfection and the real-life struggles all couples undergo at one time or another. Too often the books don't really help because they only foster the frustration caused by discrepancies between the ideal and the real.

Now, please don't misunderstand what we are saying here. Ideals are not bad in themselves; we all need something to work for. But the trouble comes when in our idealism we fail to make room for reality. Often, in the church's attempt to preserve and strengthen the institution of marriage, it has raised expectations to such a level that even the best of marriages can't deliver what is demanded. It has paradoxically weakened the very institution it wants to protect.

In our view, the church cannot call upon the people of God to keep rather than divorce their mates and not at the same time help them accept the ongoing realities of being human.

The ironic thing is that the Bible itself is the most realistic of documents. It holds forth high ideals, but it also spends a lot of time teaching how we can handle those situations where the ideal runs head-on into the real. If we could all live up to even biblical ideals all the time, why would we need a Savior, anyway?

At this point there is a fascinating parallel between what it means to be married and what it means to be a Christian.

Many of our sermons and books about living the Christian life center upon the ideal of "pressing for the mark of the high calling of God in Christ Jesus." How many times have we been challenged to reach for the very best for God? Now, there's nothing wrong with such a challenge. But the problem comes when we are promised—either explicitly or implicitly—that in exchange for all this dedication, we will be given what we want.

In this popular view, life is a quid pro quo of dedication: *If we meet his ideals, he will meet our ideals.* And the natural but regrettable corollary is that if our ideals aren't met, God has fallen down on his part of the bargain.

Over the years each of us has interacted both personally and professionally with Christians who are flat-out mad at God. When you probe their reasons, almost always they respond with a litany of complaints having to do with their disappointment with God. They resemble King David when he complains in some of the psalms that God has abandoned him to his enemies. The bottom line is usually, "God has blown it. I've done all that I know to do, and he hasn't rescued me from my problems."

Unfortunately, for them, the reality of the Christian life just doesn't match the ideal they have been promised. Life for many Christians is marked by illness, turmoil, heartache, frustration, and disillusionment—just as it is for many non-Christians. If the Christian life is seen as an idealistic quid pro quo, then when it doesn't seem to balance out, we have a right to bail out. We did our part—where is God?

Such are the perceptions of the Christian life in a narcissistic culture which focuses upon the needs of the individual as paramount. We think of God as existing to meet our needs rather than of ourselves as existing to glorify him.

The reality is that there is a cost to discipleship. The nature of the costliness of being a committed Christian will vary from person to person. But the Bible makes it clear that there *will be persecution,* in one form or another. Unfortunately, in our culture this truth is often forgotten.

In the same way that our narcissistic culture can idealize the Christian life and bring us to a place where we focus primarily on our own needs, a narcissistic approach to marriage can cause us to focus our marriages solely upon our own needs. We simply exchange a theological quid pro quo for a marital one.

Rather than renegotiate the ideals of marriage in light of reality, our dominant culture encourages us to "tear up" the person we are married to and to keep the pictures. Too often, the church's answer has been to foster larger than life pictures rather than to help the people of God to deal with what exists in fact.

Not everybody can and should have a "total marriage." Not everybody can and should have the same kind of marriage. But the facts are that real marriage is satisfying in itself, as is a discipled relationship with God through Jesus Christ. Neither is easy. Both demand work. Probably we would all agree that if one is to be a disciple of Jesus Christ it is good to "count the cost" because following him will be costly. There is a "costliness" to being married as well. Our call to reality is meant to be a call of "costliness."

Our intent in this book, then, is to base our picture of marriage on real life and not on some ideal outside or above it. It *is* attainable and it *is* workable. Marriage can be romantic, but more often the greatest meaning in marriage comes from the satisfaction of living it as a real person with another real person.

CHAPTER TWO

The Mystery of Intimacy

"It was over before it ever got started." The words barely tumbled out of her mouth before she began to cry. A young woman in her early thirties, she had always thought of herself as being able to work out her problems on her own. But now she had come seeking counsel about her troubled marriage.

"I think it was the third night of our honeymoon when I realized something was wrong. I had taken a bath after a long and busy day. I decided I would put on my very sexiest nightgown, light some candles, and then see what developed.

"I walked into the sitting room of the cottage where we were staying, and he was watching Monday Night Football. He didn't even see me; in fact, he ignored me. I got so mad that I stood right in front of the TV, and all he did was chew me out because he missed a great play. 'Thank goodness for replays,' he said.

"I was crushed. I went into the bedroom, locked the door, and cried myself to sleep. I think he slept on the couch. I guess the marriage went downhill from there."

She told the story as if it had happened yesterday, when, in fact, it had happened twelve years earlier.

To her that night had come to symbolize the rejection, emptiness, and loneliness she had felt through the years. Yet she had hung on for longer than she had thought was possible, if only for the sake of two children.

His story is markedly different.

"I can't imagine I would ever turn down an opportunity to have sex, even for Monday Night Football." His forced laugh betrayed his embarrassment.

"Probably what happened was that she started nagging me about something and I just turned off. She's been nagging me from the very beginning, and I've been turned off by it every time from the very beginning."

As he sat in the counselor's office, his entire demeanor was one of defensiveness. For him, the very idea that she was still hitting him over the head with something that had happened more than ten years before was beyond him. He was weary of being the "bad guy" in every argument. What puzzled him more was that no matter how hard he tried, he couldn't seem to make headway in terms of her criticisms of him. And so he had stopped trying.

How is it possible that two seemingly mature and intelligent adults can get themselves into a position where their marriage teeters on the brink of divorce? Why can't they be close to one another when they want to be close? These are hard questions. And they deserve answers.

We began this chapter on intimacy with this case study because it strikes at the heart of an issue that occupies the attention of every man and woman trying to work out their marriage in real life. Most of us want intimacy in our significant relationships. But sometimes the harder we try, the worse it gets.

In our opinion, part of the problem lies with the myth

that genuine intimacy is easy to come by, when it isn't. Our hope is that in this chapter we can demonstrate both why it's difficult and what can be done about it.

To begin with, most people have a rather informal but pervasive definition of what they think intimacy is, even if they haven't thought their definition through. In fact, the pursuit of intimacy has become the dominant theme of most marriages in the 1980s, especially for those couples who are in their thirties and forties.

Why, then, with all the emphasis, is there so much frustration? Our answer is that whatever intimacy in marriage is, it is much more complex than most of the quick-fix marriage manuals propose.

The Friendship Factor

Why do some relationships last when others don't? No matter how we interpret the statistics, more marriages are failing now than at any other time in human history. Although there are many reasons (more than we can deal with here), we'd like to suggest that one reason has to do with the goals we set for ourselves in terms of the marital relationship. What do we want, really?

Even a superficial evaluation of modern marital expectations as reflected in literature, film, and television indicates that intimacy is the goal for most of us. In turn, these exaggerated reflections become the standards by which we measure our performance.

What happens, however, if these contemporary expectations are flawed at their very root rather than based upon what real people, especially Christian people, can deliver? We suggest that the result is the disillusionment that many good, solid, and potentially enduring Christian marriages are facing. We define our ideal—in this case intimacy— according to values that are shaped by the standards of the culture rather than the standards of Scripture, and then we despair at the results.

The issue of intimacy in marriage may be approached from at least three directions.

The first direction is that of passion or desire. If intimacy is primarily erotic, then when the passion in a relationship is gone or even if it wanes, intimacy can be said to have been lost. This seems to be the most common contemporary interpretation of intimacy—especially in the media. When the passion in a marital relationship lessens, then it's time to move on to another relationship. The sequence can be endless.

The second direction would be that of sacrifice or duty. This seems to be the interpretation in much Christian literature, which has focused upon the biblical word *agape*. "Husbands, love your wives, as Christ loved the church and gave himself up for her" (Eph. 5:25).

Paul's exhortation in his letter to the Ephesians is held up as the highest and greatest example of what marriage is supposed to be—as the deepest form of intimacy.

But is duty enough? What happens when the sacrifice seems endless? Our observation is that what usually happens is paradoxical; endless sacrifice as the ideal provokes a result opposite from what is intended. The couple becomes increasingly alienated from one another and gives up trying to achieve intimacy. And when they do, more often than not, they give up on their marriage as well.

A third direction from which we can approach the issue of intimacy in marriage is that of friendship. In some ways, friendship can be seen as the mature fruit of a life together spent in the pursuit of common goals. Such was the case between Jesus and his disciples. We see this reflected in John's account of the words Jesus spoke in the upper room the night before he was crucified. His words describe a new kind of maturity of relationship that had evolved between them. He called them "friends."

"Greater love has no man than this, that a man lay down his life for his *friends*. You are my *friends* if you do what I command you. No longer do I call you servants, for the servant does not know what his master is doing; but I have called you *friends,* for all that I have heard from my Father I have made known to you" (John 15:13–15, emphasis added).

What we are suggesting is that, in terms of understanding intimacy, the idea of friendship allows for a fullness that neither passion and desire nor sacrifice and duty allows. It allows a relationship to form itself around the shared goals and expectations of the persons in the relationship, to the degree and at the level they are able to function. Part of being a friend is accepting the other for what he or she is, and not what we wish he or she would be. Simply put, friendship is based upon reality.

Passion, desire, sacrifice, and duty are part of what is involved in marriage—but they are not *all* that is involved. The implications of the friendship model for marriage are significant. There are just some ways you never treat a friend, and there are some ways you can be expected to treat him or her.

A Model of Friendship

If friendship is one way to envision a mature goal for marriage, where do we look for examples? We believe the friendship model of intimacy is beautifully illustrated by the relationship between Jonathan and David depicted in the Old Testament:

> Jonathan became one in spirit with David. . . . And Jonathan made a covenant with David because he loved him as himself. Jonathan took off the robe he was wearing and gave it to David, along with his tunic, and even his sword, his bow and his belt (1 Sam. 18:1–4, NIV).

You may wonder why we have chosen a friendship between two men as a model for healthy marital intimacy. (We are definitely not trying to hint at a homosexual relationship between David and Jonathan!)

In the first place, there are not that many detailed examples of marriage relationships in the Bible. But more important, we have picked a friendship between two people of the same sex to illustrate our assertion that intimacy *can* and *must* be thought of as operating beyond the boundaries of sexuality. After years of observation and experience, we've come to the conclusion that intimacy in marriage must be based on a person's ability to form intimate friendships, not only on the ability to function erotically. It is the difference between the Bible's use of the term *philos* (that is, a relationship based upon friendship) and our culture's uses of the term *eros* (that is, a relationship based upon sexual passion).

The Bible story says that "Jonathan became one in spirit with David." The Revised Standard Version says Jonathan's soul was *knit* to David's. What does it mean to be knit to another person? Most of all it means to be committed to him or her. Because Jonathan was committed to David, he made a covenant with him. And he sealed that covenant with a symbolic act, each aspect of which demonstrates on a practical level what intimacy of friendship is really like. Jonathan removed his robe, his tunic, his sword, his bow, and his belt. He then gave them all to David as a gesture of friendship. An examination of the significance of each of these items provides us with a metaphor of what is involved in the complex concept we call intimacy.

Jonathan's Robe

The robe of the son of the king was typically resplendent and decorative. It was a symbol of Jonathan's status as royalty.

Jonathan had enjoyed a life of privilege, comfort, and recognition. David was a commoner whose life, though peaceful, had been more simple and obscure. Where Jonathan walked, crowds would have gathered. David would have gone unnoticed.

Status is an interesting phenomenon. It has something to do with where a person fits on the ladder of life in terms of recognition. In our culture, the status of a marriage is usually determined by the husband's achievements in the outside world. Frequently the position of the wife is determined by the position of the husband. Only rarely is the situation reversed.

What happens, however, if one spouse fails to meet the other's expectations in terms of status? This issue has to do with the relative value of their shared *robe*.

For example, what happens if a wife fails to keep up with the upward mobility of the husband? He's moving up the corporate ladder and she's the same stay-at-home, aproned woman he married. And she's uncomfortable with the social demands of his new job. All of the women at the office dress well. She doesn't. They're attractive and seductive. She's not. They attend the latest plays and eat at sushi bars. She reads Harlequin novels and spends her energies on preparing home-cooked meals—which he may miss because of the long hours he keeps.

Or suppose the wife had it in her mind when she married that her husband would be a hard-charging, hard-driving success. Instead, he has been passed over time after time for promotions, perhaps because he doesn't try hard enough or because he isn't ambitious enough and won't pay the price to get ahead—or maybe he's just reached the limits of his ability. In either case, her worst fears have been confirmed; he's gone about as high as he will ever go. That's it. No bigger houses. No nicer cars. No trips to Europe. She'll never travel first class—if she ever gets to travel at all.

Status, you see, has pragmatic consequences. In terms of real-life marriage, the decision to marry a certain man or woman involves long-range goals as well as short-range passions. What this means to us is that when we marry, we yoke our status needs and goals to the reality of the person we marry.

Sometimes, as in the examples we've considered, a phenomenon called "differential growth" occurs. Real pain in a relationship occurs when one spouse outgrows the other.

When faced with this differential growth, a couple must make one of several decisions if they are to stay married.

The reality that must be faced is whether or not it is reasonable to expect the spouse who has "fallen behind" to change—to try to "catch up." Catching up involves two decisions: the spouse who is "behind" must decide to work harder to meet the expectations of the other spouse who is "ahead," and the one who is ahead must decide to be patient with the progress of the one who is behind.

However, other decisions are possible. The couple can decide to live with the differential—that is, the distance between them—and accept the realities that result. Or the upwardly mobile spouse can decide to lower his or her horizons and live with what "is" rather than focusing upon what might be; status needs and goals can be evaluated in light of other priorities.

What is of greatest importance is that both partners in a marriage recognize and evaluate their status quotient in terms of their marriage. They share the same "robe." And because they do, much of their happiness together as a couple is determined by their acceptance of its relative grandeur. A couple's "robe," or status, is a garment that is to be worn by the one who is privileged as well as by the one who is the commoner. Intimacy comes when they share their destinies before God.

Jonathan's Tunic

In contrast with the robe, the tunic was the garment designed to provide protection, warmth, and comfort. Probably it was made of a soft woolen fabric that protected its wearer from both cold and rain. In the act of giving his to David, Jonathan yielded his physical comfort to David.

In terms of intimacy in marriage, we have noticed that in many marriages one person tends to be the "nurture giver" and the other the "nurture getter." One person wears the tunic, and the other makes sure that it's cleaned and pressed. The difficulty comes at the point of this imbalance.

In terms of real-life marriage, whereas status is commonly a function of the husband's position, the issue of nurture and care-giving is commonly assigned to the woman in the relationship.

At a practical level, it strikes us that much dissatisfaction in a marriage, especially from the perspective of the wife, comes when the wife is expected to provide the only and constant nurture and support of the husband. The unspoken agreement seems to be that he provides the money and she provides the care. (Or they both provide money and she *still* provides the care!) The problem is, who takes care of her? And even more important, who nurtures the marriage?

In Jonathan and David's friendship, Jonathan was obviously the one with the greatest status. By all measures of what was customary, therefore, David could have been expected to defer his comfort needs for those of Jonathan. It is important to note that the opposite took place! And this was because Jonathan didn't *need* taking care of—David did. This is very important to realize.

In our own relationship, Lucy was and is the one who more often is the care-giver, while Dennis more often has been the care-getter. Realistically speaking, it is hard for Dennis to learn how to give care and nurture as well and as easily as he receives it. And many of Lucy's hurt feelings and resentments have come about because of this disparity in the relationship. Only when Dennis seriously committed himself to work on this dimension of the relationship did her resentments begin to ebb.

A very simple and recent example illustrates what we mean. Over the years, when Lucy was tired and weary, our oldest daughter, Sheryl, used to comfort her mother by grabbing a bottle of lotion and massaging her feet. (Much of Lucy's fatigue puddles in her lower extremities.) And Lucy treasured those times when she received this nurture from her daughter.

Then Sheryl went away to college. And with her leaving, the occasional foot massages ceased. It was a simple but significant loss to Lucy.

One evening, after a very demanding day at her job, Lucy mentioned to Dennis that her feet were killing her. Without much thought he offered to give her a massage. Lotion in hand, he massaged her feet and she practically purred like a kitten.

As we look back, we both remember the experience in terms of its broader meaning. Someone has to take care of the care-giver. Or, in other words, nurture should be given according to need, not according to roles or status or even inclination. There's more to a *tunic* than meets the eye.

Jonathan's Sword

This instrument was typically a short, broad weapon designed for fighting close up. Its purpose was mainly defensive. It was what a person used when the enemy got close enough to hurt. Giving a sword away meant trusting the other person enough to give up your defensive weapon.

Every person has a protective device they use when the going gets rough. For example, in our relationship Lucy's *sword* is her sarcasm. You can tell when she's threatened, because her words and tone of voice become sharp and cutting. Dennis's *sword* is yelling; when he's threatened his voice tends to rise several decibels.

For at least the first half of our marriage, each of us would use the weapons of sarcasm and shouting when in the heat of battle. But now we seem to have moved to a different style of disagreement. We are more likely to try to reason our way through an argument. We still have our fights, but they don't go on for hours like they used to, and almost always they end amicably. The net effect on our relationship is a much greater level of comfort.

What explains the change? Probably we're in a different place developmentally. Neither of us has the time or the energy to sustain the conflict as in the past. We've matured, or the years have worn the sharp edges down.

But another explanation is that a level of trust has developed between us. We have weathered some hard times together both in terms of life in general and in terms of our relationship. And as a result, we have reached the point that we trust one another with our weaknesses as well as our strengths—we trust enough to give up our precious defensive weapons. (We must admit there are times when we still reach for our *swords*—nobody's perfect in a real-life marriage—but we do it a lot less frequently than we used to!)

Jonathan's Bow

The *bow*, with its arrows, was a warrior's primary offensive weapon; it gave him the ability to inflict damage during conflict. Typically, the bow and the arrow kept the enemy at a distance. The more accurate you were as an archer, the better able you were to hurt without being hurt.

Our application of this principle involves the realization that after a period of time, every person in a marriage accumulates enough information about the other person to really do some damage if it is used against him or her. However important or however trivial the information, its potential as a weapon is what matters.

We know of several couples in which one partner brings up information from the past time after time in order to hurt the other. In one case it involves an affair which is long over, but still available (and frequently used) as a weapon. In another case it involves an abortion that resulted in the wife's infertility. Whenever heavy-duty conflict arises in the marriage, the husband throws in the wife's face her decision to abort. She is forced time after time to deal again not only with the memory of the abortion but with the grief over her loss of fertility. An affair and an abortion—two arrows within arm's reach, ready to be used to inflict harm in the heat of marital battle.

One can easily see that the purpose of a bow and its arrows is to create distance between the combatants. The reasonable decision one makes when confronted with a spouse's offensive weapons and his or her intention of using them is to

35

move out of reach. Distance usually occurs in a marriage relationship not because of the presence of the bow and arrow, but because of the experience of its being used before and the fear it will be used again.

Jonathan's Belt

The belt Jonathan gave David was the girdle that wrapped around his waist, tucked between his legs, and then tied at the back. Ultimately it held the rest of the outfit together, including the armor. Without the belt, then, the warrior was completely vulnerable.

In a day and age when assassination was common, removing one's belt and giving it to another constituted the final act of trust and openness between them. It meant the giver was genuinely at risk in the presence of the other—they were friends in the deepest and closest sense of the word.

That kind of vulnerability is the final and most important mark of the miracle of intimacy. It involves surrendering to another our status and comfort, our defensiveness and protectiveness, our ability and choice to inflict hurt and damage. And it means sharing with another person that which holds us all together—those secrets about ourselves which can hurt us the most if the other person chooses to use them. We don't mean to imply that such vulnerability is meant to be the steady state of the relationship. We are suggesting, however, that a relationship can come to a point of practical maturity which, in turn, results in a vulnerability toward one another. Given a chance, vulnerability, which is the primary ingredient of intimacy, develops as a natural byproduct of a growing relationship.

Intimacy is more than a cliché. It can be risky, and it definitely involves hard work. Sometimes it comes only after much pain or discomfort. And, typically, it occurs when you least expect it to happen—when you're most empty and vulnerable. No wonder we find it so seldom even when we want it so much. There's more to it than meets the eye.

Barriers to Intimacy

We began the chapter with a case study of a couple on the brink of divorce. What was at stake had something to do with a common struggle in the area of intimacy. What can we discern from the story that would help us understand what was going on? What made the quality of their relationship as husband and wife different from that which existed between Jonathan and David? The questions that we ask are the kind of questions Dennis asks as a therapist when faced with couples who are seeking help with their marriage.

In this case study, it was understandable that the wife was angry; no one likes to be rejected sexually. But one wonders why she gave up so easily. Was there something in her early bonding patterns that later led her to be especially vulnerable? Does she feel uncomfortable about her ability to sustain a close relationship with a significant male?

She certainly had some communication problems; she couldn't just assert herself and say directly what she wanted. Instead she depended upon nonverbal communication, however obvious, to get her point across.

When her feelings were hurt, she chose not to work the conflict through; instead, she ran for the bedroom. No wonder she struggles with intimacy.

One also wonders about the husband's early bonding experiences with women. Has he been programmed to experience significant women as controlling and demanding? Did he hide behind the football game for the same reason she ran from the room? Is he afraid of closeness?

He, too, had some problems expressing what he wanted (he wanted to watch football) and used sarcasm when he was interrupted. And he failed to express what really was bothering him (her nagging). How long had his resentment been building? Finally, his conflict-resolution skills were not very sharp. Instead of following his wife to the bedroom and working the problem out, he just sighed and slept on the couch—hoping the problem would go away. Obviously, this couple had a complex problem needing the intervention of a trained professional. Still, their struggle illustrates something about the kinds of issues that get in the way of intimacy.

And so we have two relationships—one that works and one that doesn't. What explains the difference? And more important, how can a couple who are having difficulties achieve a deeper degree of intimacy? Can married people become better friends? We will address these questions in the next chapter.

CHAPTER THREE

The Anatomy of a Mystery

In the last chapter, we looked at intimacy in relationships based on a friendship model. And we described two relationships: one that worked in terms of this model and one that didn't.

The question is, what makes one work and the other not? More important, how can a relationship work better in terms of heightened intimacy?

Our response is to delve a little deeper into what we have chosen to all the "mystery" of intimacy. What makes it mysterious? We will reach into the fields of psychology and communication for some clarification.

But a few items are worth mentioning before we continue. First of all, intimacy, according to our understanding, is a process. It's not a "thing." You can't find it on a shelf. It doesn't come in the form of a pill that you can take, and you can't pour it from a bottle. It is a process that happens when the right conditions exist. In fact, if the right conditions exist, you can't keep it from happening!

The fact that intimacy is a process also means that it's not a final destination. The last thing we want to do is to set up another set of impossible standards for intimacy that a couple in a real-life marriage can never reach! Most couples *can* improve their level of marital intimacy and build their relationship toward the model of friendship. But you will probably never reach the place where you suddenly realize, "We've arrived." The process of intimacy just doesn't work that way!

Actually, in this chapter, we will be talking about *two* developmental processes that are closely interrelated. In the first part of this chapter, we will be concerned with how an individual develops the capacity for intimacy. It is important to understand that not everyone comes to a marriage with the same ability to form and maintain intimate relationships.

But this doesn't mean we are stuck with the past when it comes to intimacy; most of us can also draw on our understanding of this developmental process to build a greater degree of intimacy into our lives together. In the latter part of this chapter we will suggest some ways couples can do this.

The Building Blocks of Intimacy

How do human beings develop the capacity to develop and maintain intimate relationships? It starts way back at the beginning—in childhood.

According to our understanding, the capacity for intimacy is developmental in nature—that is, each of its component parts builds upon the other in stairstep fashion. The technical word for this is *epigenetic*.

Figure 1 illustrates our understanding of this building process. As you can see from the diagram, each step in

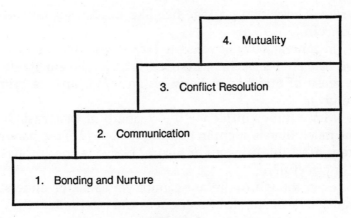

Figure 1
The Building Blocks of Intimacy

the process builds upon the next one. The capacity to develop intimate relationships is the result of a process that begins with the earliest experiences of an infant. And it is a cumulative process—that is, what goes before forms the basis of what comes later in life.

This is similar to many other processes in human development. For example, most children learn to read when they are in the first two or three years of school. If they don't learn to read during those years, their progress through school—and life—may be hindered.

In other words, the kind of reader one is today has something to do with how well reading was learned as a child. And in the same way, the quality of one's intimate relationships today has something to do with the quality of intimate relationships that have gone before. That is why it is worth going back to the beginning in exploring the question of intimacy.

Bonding and Nurture: The Foundation for Intimacy

As we have said, our first and primary intimate relationships affect our subsequent ones. And especially important to those early relationships are the elements of *bonding* and *nurture.* These two go together like heads and tails of the same coin.

In general, *bonding* refers to *the sense of connectedness that exists between people.* In terms of early development, it refers to the sense of attachment between an infant and its primary care-giver.

Many things influence the strength of that basic bond. How much time is spent in holding the baby? Is the parent (or parent substitute) anxious or secure? Nervous or calm? Resentful or grateful?

Even though the infant cannot yet speak or understand language, he or she still experiences and internalizes the quality of the relationship and feels "connected" to a greater or lesser degree. And this sense of connectedness (or lack of it) becomes a kind of filter through which the infant experiences later intimate relationships. A child who is strongly bonded to his or her earliest care-giver will find it easier to attach himself or herself in later relationships.

Nurture, in turn, refers to *the quality of the care a person or relationship receives.* And just as the strength of the basic bond can vary, so can the nature of the care.

Psychologist Erich Fromm referred to two basic kinds of nurture as "milk and honey." When talking about mother love, for instance, Fromm said that almost all mothers are able to provide for their infants' basic physical needs. He referred to this kind of care as the "milk" of mother love. But some mothers are able to go beyond the basics and provide for their children's emotional needs—to give them a sense of the sweetness of life. He referred to this kind of nurture as "honey."

Obviously, the best kind of nurture would involve both. But for a number of reasons, some children grow up having experienced the bread but not the jam, the milk but not the honey. And this can limit their capacity to develop future relationships that function on an emotional level.

For what begins as bonding and nurture in a child's early experience eventually develops into the ability to relate to others with a sense of trust and openness. People who as infants develop a strong sense of attachment to those they love and who feel confident that their physical and emotional needs will be met carry that sense of attachment and confidence all through life, and they bring it to their later relationships. Out of that context begins the mystery of intimacy.

Communication—A Relational Necessity

Bonding and nurture form the foundational building block for developing a capacity for intimacy. But as children grow up, they need more than the feeling of being attached and cared for. They also need to learn communication with those who are important in their lives.

Now, when we speak of communication here, we aren't just talking about language development—although learning to communicate certainly involves learning to use words skillfully. Rather, we are talking about communication in its relational context—how language affects the relationship between persons.

In our view, relational *communication* involves *the freedom and ability to express what you feel and think, with the confidence that you will be heard and responded to with some degree of consistency and maturity.* When children have internalized that freedom and that confidence, they have learned sound relational communication.

This description of good communication breaks down into four components:

1. freedom and ability to express oneself,
2. awareness of feelings and thoughts,
3. confidence that one will be heard and responded to,
4. confidence that this hearing and response will be done with some degree of consistency and maturity.

Let's look at each of these components in turn in order to understand better how good relational communication skills develop (or don't develop).

A sense of having *the freedom to express oneself* begins very early in life. For children almost from the beginning learn to measure their approach to their primary care-givers according to the responses they receive.

Small infants, for example, are limited in their ability to communicate, but even their crying is an attempt to say something. And the primary care-giver's response says something back—ideally, "You will be taken care of." The process of interaction between the two forms the blueprint for later communication skills.

The message a tiny infant needs to hear is, "If you let me know you have a need, I will see that your need is met." (At this very early point, communication ties in very closely with bonding and nurture.) But as verbal skills develop, the message becomes more complex. A healthy pattern of communication between parent and child will eventually include making it clear that, although the child is free to express his or her needs, there are certain reasonable limits.

That is, children who learn good communication will internalize the message that they are important, but that they are not the center of the universe. They will learn that it is always appropriate to express what they want or don't want, need or don't need, yet with the full understanding that the parent's response may be based upon factors or conditions beyond the child's control.

If the parents' own communication skills are faulty, they can sometimes send messages they don't intend to send, and children may learn some faulty communication lessons.

For example, children can get the message that they can demand anything at any time and someone will respond immediately. Or they can get the idea that they will only be loved if they are "good"—that is, quiet and not expressive about their needs. Or they can learn that the response they receive is erratic and unpredictable and has no clear relationship to the child's needs or desires—therefore there is no point in expressing themselves. Children who internalize these messages will probably tend to apply them to later relationships, too—and those later relationships will probably suffer from communication problems.

The freedom to express oneself is critical to the ability to foster intimacy in any relationship. For intimacy involves both giving and getting—as well as *knowing* what you have to give and what you want to get. The freedom to be expressive forms a kind of bracket within which this giving and getting can take place.

The second component for communication is *awareness of feelings and thoughts.* The order in which these two elements are listed is deliberate. For although the two are equally important, developmentally and psychologically speaking, feelings come first. Every person begins life as very much a feeling person and very minimally a thinking person. Thought processes then mature as the individual matures.

Difficulties can arise in later relationships when, for one reason or another, a child is taught to reverse the order of feeling and thinking—or to exclude one or the other. It is amazing how often this is done—and the effect on the level of intimacy is considerable.

At the practical level, for example, the person who has been taught to deal with the world in terms of "thinking first" tends to deal with people in terms of "thinking only." And in any relationship, when closeness and openness are needed and desired, nothing can stifle intimacy more quickly than denying the validity of feelings.

Why? Because feelings are more primal, and can't be changed by the application of reason.

For example, suppose a child awakens in the night because of a nightmare involving ghosts. When she awakens, she's terrified that there are ghosts in the closet. Responding to her cries, her father sits at the side of the bed and tries to reason with the child:

"Let me explain to you why ghosts can't possibly exist . . ."

But is the child any less frightened after such a reasoned approach? No. You can bet that if the child were taken by the hand and led to the closet after the father's explanation, her adrenaline would flow and her heart would beat faster. Why? Because the feelings of the child are real, even though they are irrational. And those feelings need to be dealt with before reason can have any effect.

The much more effective approach, then, would be for the father to hold the child and assure her that he will protect her. Only then would she be ready to hear his explanation about why ghosts aren't real.

The basic principle for communication must always be: Deal with the feelings first, and then explain. Trying to put thought first can lead to communication breakdowns and problems in maintaining intimate relationships.

But "feelings first" can be equally dysfunctional if it leads to dealing with the world in terms of "feelings only." In a child, the result can be tantrums and inappropriate and excessive demands. In adult relationships, a feelings-first approach can lead to emotional and relational cut-offs and intimidation.

Good communication involves the freedom to be appropriately expressive of both how you feel and what you think. What is needed for healthy intimacy to occur is the acceptance of both. And this is best learned very early in life.

The third component of communication is *confidence in being heard and responded to.* And how well this confidence is developed in a child depends to a great extent on both what and how the parent or care-giver communicates.

Modern communication theory holds that you cannot *not* communicate; all behavior communicates something. Whether it is verbal or nonverbal, explicit or implicit, obvious or subtle, what you say and how you say it sends a message to the hearer. The *what* in communication is the message. *How* it is said is called the "metamessage."

The metamessage involves what you *don't say,* as well. The absence of a verbal message can be as significant as the presence of one in that the very lack of a message forms an implicit metamessage. Or nonverbal behavior can send a metamessage that contradicts what is said verbally. When patterns of behavior consistently contradict verbal messages, confusion results, and eventually the metamessage overwhelms the message.

For example, if you were never held as a child or told that you were loved, the absence of words and touch formed a message in and of itself. If you were told that your father loves you, but he was rarely there when you knew he could be, the verbal message of love was contradicted by the metamessage of neglect.

This explains why many people feel unimportant, even though no one has ever *said* they were unimportant. The metamessages they received and internalized as children are subsequently reexperienced as adults. And their ability to maintain healthy communication in an intimate relationship may suffer accordingly.

In contrast, children who receive congruent messages and metamessages of love and support grow up secure in the belief that they are important enough to be listened to and responded to. In turn, they find it easier to establish intimate relationships with others.

The last component of communication involves the *consistency* and *maturity* of those who hear and respond. In the case of early development, this depends on the character and behavior of the parent or care-giver.

Consistency has to do with dependability and predictability. A child who feels confident that the significant people in his or her life will be there when they are needed—and that they will bring with them some degree of stability—develops a strength that will help him or her maintain intimate relationships later. But a child who has to worry about how dependable those significant people are will probably have some problems in later relationships.

Maturity has to do with the child's recognition that he or she can safely be a child because the parents themselves don't need parenting. There is an appropriate place for childishness and foolishness, and the child can trust the parent to allow, even encourage, spontaneity and freedom while simultaneously setting limits for that spontaneity.

In a developmental sense, the child's dependence upon the parents' maturity allows the child to express his or her own immaturity within boundaries set by the parents. The end result for the child is the experience of freedom within limits. This dimension of communication establishes the ability to be spontaneous and creative, qualities which contribute to the "honey" in a person's soul and add sweetness to intimate relationships.

Conflict Management—Working Things Out

The third building block in the development of intimacy, is *conflict management.* This is more than a specialized form of communication; it involves learning to relate to others as an equal and with parity.

Any two people who have learned to communicate eventually come into conflict. How can those differences be resolved? Are the differences resolved by a set of givens, such as "men rule women" and "children should be seen and not heard"? Or are they resolved with an eye to reciprocity, or the need for both people to stay "with it" in a give-and-take kind of way until the problem is solved?

How we learn to handle conflict in our early lives inevitably affects our ability to handle intimacy. Conflict engenders hurt feelings. In turn, hurt feelings inhibit closeness. Unless and until we learn to work through conflict, the presence of hurt and anger inhibits the openness that is necessary for intimacy.

What is a healthy way to "work through conflict"? We recommend a method of conflict resolution which simultaneously embodies both a goal and a process—a method suggested by Roger Fisher in his excellent book, *Getting to Yes.* * It has to do with deciding that for the most part in order to be constructive every conflict must end up in a "win/win" situation.

*Roger Fisher and William Ury, *Getting to Yes: Negotiationg Agreement without Giving In* (Boston: Houghton Mifflin, 1981).

According to Fisher, there are four common positions of conflict resolution. The first position often taken in families is to *ignore an issue,* hoping that it will go away. Usually this means that one partner or the other (usually the same one consistently) just gives up without even raising the issue. Fisher calls this a "lose/win" situation. If a person knows something is wrong and chooses to "let it go" or "forget about it," he or she almost guarantees that the issue will surface again in more strident terms—or that the relationship will stagnate because important issues are never addressed. Ignoring problems doesn't make them go away.

A second position is to *live with a problem.* This can be seen as a "lose/lose" option. "Live with it" differs from "ignore it" in that the family decides to tolerate the conflict as a steady state of the relationship. Neither party wins, but neither party is happy or satisfied. Under such conditions, it's usually not long before the conflict erodes family relationships in the same way that uncontrolled runoff erodes a hillside. The end result is both ugly and useless.

The third position is to *go to war.* Fisher calls this option a "win/lose" situation. Under these conditions, a couple draws the battle lines in such a way as to guarantee that one person will lose and one person will win—and both feel they *have to* win! With this pattern, there can be only so many losses before one or the other of the combatants calls off the relationship.

The fourth position is *getting to yes.* It is the "win/win" option. In a win/win situation, each party in the conflict has the opportunity to put all of his or her concerns on the table without having them judged or denigrated. The rules are that each person is equal and that every concern is to be addressed. Only at that point are the parties in conflict encouraged to yield when and where they can. For by then being willing to yield is seen not as losing, but as being committed to the welfare of the other. In the terminology of Scripture it is "becoming a servant."

According to Fisher, only after a couple has aired their concerns and decided when and where they are willing to yield are they ready to tackle the major issue or issues that divide them. By this point, the central issues often seem to resolve themselves.

Fisher's model for conflict management presupposes an ability to act trustingly toward one another and to communicate about both thoughts and feelings. In marriage, they are linked together.

But needless to say, many of us fail to learn to handle conflict that way when we are children. Many people never see healthy conflict management modeled in their homes— and as a result they never learn how to handle the inevitable friction that occurs in real-life marriage.

Dennis sees this all the time in counseling. A man remembers that whenever his mother tried to bring up an issue, his father would always cut her off with "I don't want to talk about it!" Or a woman remembers hiding in a closet while her parents went at each other tooth and toenail. Still another man remembers growing up in a home where unresolved issues always hung heavy in the air and family members seemed to live separate lives. And all these people are having trouble in their present relationships as a result of the way conflict was handled at home when they were children.

Some people who grow up in homes where conflict is poorly managed end up handling conflict just as their parents did. Others may overreact in the opposite direction. But most will end up having some problems with intimate relationships. (It is widely documented that the most extreme kind of poor conflict management—that resulting in physical or emotional abuse—tends to run in families; the children learn it from the parents.)

Mutuality: The Fruit of the Process

The mystery of intimacy begins with the building block of bonding and nurture, builds upon the blocks of communication and conflict resolution, and concludes with the fourth building block: *mutuality.*

Mutuality is very closely related to the capacity to make mature commitments to other people. It involves being able to live in close relationship—working and playing together. It is the logical byproduct of the process that begins with bonding and nurture, then develops further as the capacity for communication and the resolution of conflict are learned.

Now it *is* possible to proceed from one step to the next before the first step is really mastered—just as it is possible in school to be promoted from the early grades (and even graduate) without really being able to read well. For example, a person whose early bonding experiences were not fully adequate may manage to communicate, handle conflict, and live in relationship to a certain extent. But just as poor reading handicaps a student in later subjects, a problem at any one stage of development will handicap a person in future stages.

Without each of the preceding ingredients, mutuality is limited. And without mutuality, true intimacy is negligible. The ability to form a commitment and live in mutuality with another person is the mature fruit of which bonding and nurture are the seeds.

Intimacy Is a Lifetime Thing

It ought to be clear by now that we believe an individual's ability or inability to function in an intimate relationship is shaped long before that person ever enters a marriage—and that it is closely tied to how the individual learned to function in his or her earliest relationships.

Our experience both as a couple and as professionals has tended to support this conclusion. And recently published research touching upon the nature of intimacy corroborates what we are saying.

The prestigious family journal, *Family Process,*[*] recently carried a report on a fifteen-year follow-up study on a group

*Albers, Doane, and Mintz, article in *Family Process*, vol. 25, no. 3, 379–389.

of patients first interviewed in the mid-1960s by researchers at the UCLA Medical School Psychology Outpatient Clinic.

At the time of the original interviews, the patients had been troubled adolescents. And it had been determined that most of these kids' problems involved patterns of relating they had learned in their families. These families were struggling with issues of expressed emotion, communication, and areas of support and responsibility. (Note the similarity of these issues to the four building blocks.)

In the follow-up study, forty-seven of the original sixty-five patients—now adults—were located and interviewed with the purpose of discovering whether or not their poor earlier parent-child relationships had any effect upon their social competence now. And the interesting conclusion was that for the most part, those early dysfunctional relationships had *not* significantly influenced later functioning as adults: But there was one very important exception

A number of individuals. . . . have managed to establish relatively good levels of functioning in their work setting or with their friendship network. *The interesting exception to all of this is in the realm of intimate friendships.* Here it appears that early family relationships *are* correlated with long-term functioning. Individuals from families characterized as highly critical or intrusive, or with high levels of communication deviance, are more likely to have difficulty in establishing and maintaining an intimate relationship. *These people may have adequate relationships with [casual] friends, or function well at work, but they have difficulty in love relationships or marriage.* *

Granted, this study was done with disturbed individuals, but its implications for our understanding of intimacy are fairly clear. The capacity for intimacy is developed over a lifetime; it is not something we can wish into existence or coerce into being. The ability to develop and maintain inti-

*Albers, Doane, and Mintz, 387, emphasis added.

mate relationships is established early in life. And if it is *not* developed early, it is not easy to develop later.

Building More Intimacy into Your Marriage

But what's a couple to do? If the capacity for intimacy is determined early in life, is there any hope for married people who are struggling with issues of intimacy?

Of course! As implied earlier, we are not bound by the past—even if we *are* strongly influenced by it. If there were no chance of improving the level of intimacy in a marriage, there would be no point in writing this chapter!

In light of all that has been said above, we suggest the following as a kind of blueprint for how a couple can grow in their level of intimacy:

1. Look into the Past.

If much of a person's capacity for intimacy develops in childhood, it makes sense that building more intimacy into a marriage will involve looking into both partners' pasts to see if any of the basic steps were neglected.

But there may be some difficulty at this point. Although most of us can remember some early experiences that have a bearing on our present relationships, much of what goes into a person's capacity for intimacy operates at the unconscious level. How can we possibly know how we or our spouse experienced our very early years?

One answer to the dilemma is to evaluate our past relationships in light of our present ability to relate intimately to others. Paradoxically, we can begin understanding the past by focusing on the present, by asking, "How are we doing right now in our relationship?"

If both of you seem to be doing well, then it's reasonable to assume that the early foundations were probably stable and productive, or at least that you're already moving in the right direction.

However, if you are struggling, then the place to begin is with your earliest experiences. It never hurts to be honestly reflective. Think of the four developmental steps: bonding and nurture, communication, conflict resolution, and commitment. How were these things handled in your family? If other family members are available, ask them what they remember. Try to think in terms of relationships and patterns of behavior rather than in terms of events or crises.

2. Be Slow to Judge.

The tendency at this point might be to place the "blame" for relational problems on somebody in our past—especially our parents. But this is unproductive and usually unfair.

In the first place, our early perceptions—although "real" in the sense that they shape our understanding and relationships—are not always accurate in view of the actual circumstances. (For example, we might have felt neglected when actually our primary care-giver was ill and unable to care for us.) And even if our perceptions are accurate, those who taught us our early relationships were probably doing the best they could, given their own backgrounds and personalities.

The point of looking into our pasts is not to assess blame but to gain insight. We need to ask: "What can I learn about myself by understanding those who have gone before me?"— not, "What did my family do to me?"

But it's not only our parents that we tend to blame. It is also very tempting to blame our spouse for having relational difficulties in our marriage—especially if our spouse is the one who has problems with closeness.

But here it may help to remember that it is very hard to change patterns of relationship developed early in life. Blaming a marital partner for something he or she cannot help is not really fair—nor is it likely to help him or her draw closer in relationship.

Finally, it's important to remember to apply the "slow to judge" rule to yourself, too. As we have said, the intimacy issue is complex. Having a more intimate relationship requires hard work, but even working hard won't guarantee it. So forgiveness and acceptance—of yourself, your family of origin, and your spouse—become especially important.

3. Be Willing to Rebuild.

If either or both of you are having problems with intimacy because your early development was hindered in some way, it is possible to "start over" to a certain extent. This is not easy; it takes hard work and dedication. But we have seen it happen.

For intimacy develops in a marriage through basically the same process as it develops in an individual. It begins with a process of bonding—building an attachment—and nurturing—taking care of one another. It proceeds to building communication and learning conflict management. Finally, it develops a mutuality that is the basis for true intimacy.

To rebuild a capacity for intimacy, it may be necessary to go back to the point where the problems began for either one or both of you.

It might be with bonding or nurture—with attaching to and caring for one another. But there are limits at this point. Marital partners can "rebond" and provide nurture for one another, but one spouse should not be put in the position of having to be a "parent" to the other. If one partner is severely lacking in very basic bonding and nurturing experiences, professional help may be in order.

More commonly, the problem is in the areas of communication or conflict resolution. We hope some of the later chapters will help in these areas. And there are many good books on the market, such as Fisher's *Getting to Yes* and Dennis's *Thoroughly Married,** that can be useful.

*Dennis Guernsey, *Thoroughly Married* (Waco, TX: Word Books, 1984).

It should go without saying that all this involves *talking* about individual backgrounds and the present state of the marriage. But it is a constant surprise to us how seldom couples talk to each other about issues that really matter in their relationship. This is probably because many such conversations end in blaming and defensiveness—indicating some problems at the level of communication.

We suggest that you "talk through" the intimacy-building process together step by step—discussing your individual pasts and your present relationship. Try hard to do this with as much of an open and nonjudgmental spirit as you can muster—to discuss instead of blaming and to listen without becoming defensive. And don't forget to take turns.

4. Seek Help if Either of You Think You Need It.

Realistically speaking, discussions such as these can open up issues that are deeper and more hurtful than either of you imagined. If that happens, stop the discussion if you can and agree to find a person you can trust and with whom you can talk. This could be a pastor or a professional counselor or even a trusted friend—although in some cases a professional might be advisable.

Remember, seeking help is not a sign of weakness. On the contrary, it is a sign of growth and maturity. And it may be the key to helping you understand yourselves, each other, and the issue of intimacy in your marriage.

5. Take Responsibility for the Present.

Understanding the past does not excuse you from responsibility for the present. Whatever happened before is only that: something that happened before. You are responsible for what is happening now in the relationships that are most important to you.

People who did not develop intimacy skills in childhood can develop a greater capacity for intimacy in adulthood. The key is neither to blame others or to become defensive, but to become wisely evaluative—and then to take responsibility for working hard.

6. Ask for What You Want—But Be Ready to Live with What You Get.

This should be the watchword for all the issues of real-life marriage. If a couple wants a greater degree of intimacy in their marriage, they must be willing to work hard at nurturing one another, at learning to communicate and resolve conflict, at renewing their commitment to one another on ever deeper levels. And it will take two to do the work; one person can't double up and make it all happen by himself or herself.

But at the same time, it is important to remember that intimacy really is a mystery; it is not something you can force. Building the capacity for intimate relationships is not easy once a person has become an adult, and not everyone will be able to achieve (or even desire) the same levels of intimacy, especially if early relationships have been lacking.

Here again the analogy of reading may be helpful. Most people whose early reading background is less than ideal *can* learn to read later. But a few may not, and many will always have a sense of being a little behind. In the same way, marriage partners who didn't develop strong relational skills as children may not ever quite "catch up" when it comes to developing intimacy in their marriages—although they can certainly improve.

So finally, after all the work, there comes a point in any real-life marriage where the partners simply have to accept each other. There are points in every relationship where we need to ask God's help in accepting the reality of what is while at the same time continuing to work for what can be.

And it helps to remember that the joy of intimacy really is in the process as well as in the end result. Those who seek intimacy may not ever feel they have arrived. But often they will find something of what they want in the very seeking of it!

CHAPTER FOUR

Your Map or Mine?

Often what at first attracts us to one another eventually repels us. Our similarities are easy to take. Our differences aren't. Typically, the longer we are married, the less willing we are to put up with the idiosyncrasies we earlier dismissed as insignificant. The years have a way of eroding our tolerance for what once seemed unimportant. In a real marriage between real people, then, we must come to grips with how we are dissimilar, and we must learn how to cope with these differences.

This chapter is about a major source of differences between people in general and married couples in particular: representational systems. Our goal is to help you come to understand the nature of these differences and how to cope with them more effectively.

Understanding Personal Maps

It's Friday afternoon. After a hard day at the office, Tom and Marcia are on their way home. Sarah, their teenaged daughter, is already there.

Marcia arrives before Tom does and enters the house through the living room door. Immediately she takes stock of what she sees—and she doesn't like it. There are newspapers scattered around the room, shoes dropped casually at the side of the sofa, and drinking glasses left on the coffee table. The disarray is a visual offense to her—"a mess." And her immediate response is to seek out her daughter and "request" that the situation be rectified.

No sooner has she left the room than Tom opens the front door. Interestingly enough, he doesn't even notice the stuff scattered around the room; he's too distracted by the "noise" coming from Sarah's bedroom. Loud rock music is issuing from her stereo, and he can hear loud guffaws of laughter. He stalks down the hall and pounds on Sarah's door, demanding that she and her friends "knock off the noise" and "settle down."

But Sarah is indignant; she can't see what her parents are so upset about. She has just been doing what she likes to do—having fun with her friends, sitting in the cozy nest of her room and letting the sound surround her like warm water in a big bathtub.

It's true that the house is a mess according to Mom's standards and that the music is loud according to Dad's, but to Sarah everything felt great. Now, with Tom and Marcia standing at the bedroom door and barking out commands, she feels attacked and embarrassed. As far as family harmony is concerned, the situation is as potentially explosive as an underground atomic test site in Nevada.

These three people are in the same house, but each is *experiencing* it differently. And each *interprets* it differently, too—each has different ideas about what is wrong or right with the house.

How can three people experience and interpret the same

reality so differently? Because each is relying on a different *personal map* to help him or her make some sense of what is happening. And the differences in personal maps can be just as divisive in a family as differences in temperaments.

Now, when we say "maps," we're not talking about the kind we carry in the car, but the kind we carry in our heads. In this chapter we hope to show how an understanding of personal maps can help us handle our misunderstandings by clarifying some of the basic ways we are different from one another. And then we would like to look at some basic principles for handling our differences—no matter where they come from.

The Essence of Mapmaking

But just what do we mean by "personal maps"?

In its broadest sense, a "map" is a way of sorting out and interpreting experience.

A person who makes a map of a geographical area, for instance, experiences the reality of a region—roads, mountains, rainfall, population, points of interest, and so on—and then organizes that information so as to make it useful and meaningful.

A geographical region can be experienced in many different ways, of course—in terms of its landscape, its weather, its geology, the roads that transverse it. But it would be impossible to show every bit of information that exists about a region, so a mapmaker chooses to concentrate on one particular aspect of the area—its highways, for instance, or its annual rainfall or its elevation.

A map of a geographical area, then, is a mapmaker's interpretation of a region based on one particular kind of experience or information. Once it is made, the map is also a tool for experiencing that region in the future.

The same principle applies to the way we human beings experience and interpret the world around us.

We are made in such a way that we experience the world around us through our five senses: hearing, seeing, feeling (or touching), smelling, and tasting. All five senses feed a series of complex messages into our head.

But this is all raw data, and it is up to us to interpret these messages and determine their meaning. And that's where personal maps come in. Our minds interpret and organize the sensory information we receive—they "map it out" for us. And this mental map in turn becomes a tool for helping us organize further information as our senses bring it in.

When we speak of a personal map, then, we are referring to the particular way our minds sort out the sensory information we receive. Another term for this (from a body of literature known as neurolinguistics) is *representational system.*

Simply put, *personal maps or representational systems are the ways different people sort out the messages their senses send them and organize that sensory input in their minds.*

Now, just as mapmakers for a geographical region tend to specialize in one type of information, we human beings tend to "specialize" in one source of sensory input.

In other words, each of us tends to rely on one of our senses as our primary source for experiencing the world—either our sight, our hearing, or our sense of touch and feeling. (That is not to say smell and taste are not important; they simply are not the senses people tend to rely on most.)

It follows naturally that not everyone depends on the same sense. Some are "visual" people; some rely more on their auditory sense; still others depend on their sense of feeling or touch. And our personal maps vary according to what sense we use the most.

In other words, God has created us with the ability to experience our world and to interpret that world. But not all of us experience the world the same way. As a consequence, we interpret the world differently—both to ourselves and to others. And that difference can be a significant source of misunderstanding between people in a family.

Same World, Different Maps

What would happen if we put in the same fifty-square-mile area a salesman with a highway map, a farmer with a rainfall map, and a geologist with a topographic map—and asked them to pinpoint the most lucrative site for business. Would they pick the same spot? Would they even be able to communicate with one another about the region?

The same kind of thing can happen when people in a family rely on different personal maps to interpret the reality of their home and relationships.

In the example that opened the chapter, each member of the family was relying on a different sense to interpret what was going on. The mother relied mostly on her visual or seeing sense. The father relied on his auditory or hearing sense. And the teenager relied on her kinesthetic, or feeling/touching sense. No wonder they had trouble understanding each other!

The differences between their interpretations of their experience reflect the differences in their personal maps. Let's look at each of these maps a little more closely:

Visual or "Seeing" Maps

People who organize their world according to what they see are acutely aware of visual stimuli. They easily create images in their imagination or recreate a scene in vivid detail. When they want to learn something, they learn best if they can see the task performed or see it in writing. If they can see it, they've got it. Usually, they love to read. If it's written down, it's real. "Visual" people tend to love lists.

In general, these people communicate best when they' talk in pictures. That is, they are likely to describe their world using words that depict color, shape, size, and other visual details. They may not necessarily be artists, but they are able to see the bits and pieces of their world in a way that indicates an attention to detail. Typically, they have a sense of the "big picture" as well.

At the same time, "visual people" tend to operate on an "out of sight, out of mind" basis. If something is not where they can see it—or if they can't visualize it—it doesn't have much meaning for them.

Visual people also tend to be concerned with appearances; they tend to think in terms of the impressions others will draw based upon what a situation "looks" like. Propriety may be very important to them, because actions bear an image and images are significant.

Lucy is a visual person. When we were looking for a house in Pasadena, where we now work, Dennis came upon the house we now live in. When he and the real estate agent walked through the house, Dennis knew it was special but he didn't know exactly why. He returned home and struggled in vain to describe it to Lucy.

The upshot of the conversation was that the next day we drove to the house and walked through it in much the same way Dennis and the agent had done the day before. Lucy said very little; she just walked.

Afterward, standing in the street, Dennis asked, "Well, what do you think? On a scale of one to ten, what is it?"

"It's a nine," she replied. "In fact, we'll only need to buy one piece of furniture for the living room."

Dennis, who is not a visual, was flabbergasted. Lucy had pictured each piece of furniture in our old house and had placed them all in the rooms of the new house—all in her mind. When the time came to move, it all fit together like the pieces of a puzzle. Visuals can do that. Those who aren't visually oriented simply cannot.

Auditory/Tonal or "Hearing/Speaking" Maps

People who organize their world based on what they hear are very conscious of words and speech. They focus on what is said and what they hear. They love to talk and argue. They create conversations in their minds in the same way visuals create images. When it comes to learning, they love lectures. They can follow a dialogue with relative ease. If they can talk something through, they learn. Their emphasis is not only on what they hear, but also on what they say; they are listening to themselves as they speak. Once they've said it, they've got it.

As a result, hearing/speaking people are very conscious of the tone of others' voices or the inflections of their speech. They can be very aware of sarcasm or cynicism. Likewise, they are very conscious of verbal praise or criticism—even to the point of overreacting.

These kind of people tend to feel that if they said or heard something, it's real. If it wasn't said or they didn't hear it, it may not register with them. Dennis is auditory/tonal. When he was in seminary, he worked full time and carried almost a full load in school, and that made finding time to study difficult. When it came time for exams, he relied on his ability to remember the lectures and, in particular, on his regular meetings with a study group. This group of fellow students would meet together before an exam and discuss the material. Dennis found that if he could say out loud what he needed to know, he would remember it the next day. Time after time, his study group pulled him through simply by giving him the opportunity to verbalize what he needed to know.

Kinesthetic or "Feeling/Touching" Maps

The third representational system is the kinesthetic. Kinesthetics experience their world in both a visceral and a tactile way (through their "gut" and through their skin). They are very conscious of feelings, their own as well as the feelings of others. People who organize their world according to how they feel are acutely aware of the ambiance of their environment. Everything can be translated into feelings. But we are not talking about "feelings" in the sense of "emotion," but in the sense of "tuning in" on a visceral level. To a kinesthetic, images, sounds, and objects are to be experienced—"felt."

When kinesthetics want to learn something, they need to "do" it. If they can handle an object and manipulate it, they can understand it. If instructions are written out or spoken, they may get lost in the images and the words; they need to participate in the experience. This is the tactile side of their representational system.

But touch is not all that is important to kinesthetics. They usually are very tuned in to their internal, bodily response to what is going on around them. They can pick up on tension in a room, anxiety in a person's actions, or fear in another's response. Their feeling sense functions almost like an antenna when it comes to their environment. Sometimes this gets in their way. Because of their own sensitivity, they quickly and easily jump to conclusions about what others feel.

Recently, we were watching television and happened upon a program involving an interview with a famous actress. The interviewer asked the actress what made her successful. The actress was pensive for a moment and then responded that she always tried to "get into the character" she was portraying. When the interviewer pushed for an explanation, she responded in terms of her ability to "get in touch" with what the character would be feeling in a particular situation. She was able to create that experience within herself and then act it out on the stage or screen.

As the interview progressed, they took a tour of the actress's home. Each room was tastefully decorated, but what was interesting to us was that she described it to her television audience in terms of how each room *felt* to her. The living room was designed to evoke a particular feeling when she was in it. So was the bedroom, and so on.

At the end of the interview, the actress was asked why she hadn't worked in the past year. Her response was that none of the scripts that had been offered seemed right to her. And if it didn't feel right, she wasn't going to do it. She was a kinesthetic.

Identifying Your Map

All of us use all three ways of organizing our experience to one degree or another (with the obvious exception of someone who has lost the use of one sense or another). But as we have indicated, one sense tends to dominate. We each have a dominate or primary system, a secondary system or backup, and a minimal system.

In order to identify your dominant system, we suggest you begin by answering the questions in the "Identifying Your Map" (figure 1) chart. When you have finished all the questions, total up your "yes" answers. Based on these totals, try to identify which is your dominant system—the one with the most "yeses." The one with the fewest yeses would then be your minimal system, and the one in the middle would be your backup.

Remember, you are only trying to get an idea of how you are similar to and different from to those around you—not to put yourself in a category or box. So don't try to be too exact or belabor the point. Just try to get a feel for how you tend to experience reality.

Then, ask someone who knows you well to answer the same questionnaire about you. Compare your answers with your estimate. This should help you be a little more objective.

If You Can't Decide . . .

If you are having difficulty deciding which is your representational system, ask your friend to observe you over the next few days. By closely observing the language you use, this person can give you some clues to what your representational system is.

The assumption (according to neurolinguists) is that our choice of words, though unconscious most of the time, is not random; there are representational reasons behind what we say. And so we will tend to use words that reflect the sense we rely on most. For example, a visual person will tend to use

ARE YOU A VISUAL?

When you imagine yourself talking with others, do you create visual images in your mind as you talk? Do you "see" the encounter taking place? yes___ no___

As you listen to others, are you easily distracted by what you see—the look on the speaker's face, his or her appearance, and so on? yes___ no___

At the end of a conversation, are your memories based on what you have seen? yes___ no___

When it comes to learning something new, does seeing the material displayed on a chalkboard or reading about it help you significantly? yes___ no___

When it comes to remembering details, are you likely to recreate the situation or object as a picture in your head and then use that picture as a means of remembering? yes___ no___

Is it easy for you to visualize where you are in a geographical area by studying a road map?

ARE YOU AN AUDITORY/TONAL?

When you imagine talking with others, do you have the conversation first in your head? yes___ no___

As you listen to others, are you easily distracted by the tone or sound of their voice? yes___ no___

At the end of a conversation, are your memories based on what you have heard or said? yes___ no___

When it comes to learning something new, are you helped significantly by being able to listen to the instructions or to talk about them with others? yes___ no___

Are your memories of past events likely to be memories of what you heard or said? yes___ no___

Do you tend to ask directions when visiting a new geographical area? yes___ no___

ARE YOU A KINESTHETIC?

When you anticipate talking to others, do you often experience any kind of physical sensation such as knot in your stomach? yes___ no___

As you listen to others, are you easily distracted either by what you are feeling inside or by what you think the other person is feeling? yes___ no___

Do you find it difficult to remember details about exactly what you heard or what you saw? yes___ no___

Do you learn best in a "hands on" situation? yes___ no___

Do you remember intensely how you felt about past events or situations? yes___ no___

When you get lost, are you likely to wander around until you find your way? yes___ no___

Figure 1
Identifying Your Map

words that refer to seeing; an auditory person, words relating to hearing, and so forth.

Have the person who is watching you keep track of the words you use in your everyday conversation. Then, after a few days, ask him or her what he or she thinks your dominant system is. Compare your observer's conclusion with your own estimate.

To give the observer an indication of what to look for, here are some commonly used words and the representational system they signify:

Visual	Auditory	Kinesthetic
see	hear	feel
focus	listen	touch
clear	talk	firm
bright	yell	pressure
picture	noisy	tense
show	discuss	hurt
hazy	call	clumsy
pretty	shout	pushy
glimpse	harmony	relax
look	blast	irritate

The rule for deciding where a word fits is to ask which representational system has to be used in order for the message or meaning of the word to be duplicated. For example, "yell" suggests a speaking or auditory/tonal meaning. "Pushy" suggests a tactile or kinesthetic meaning. After a day or two, the direction you are leaning in terms of a dominant representational system will probably become clear.

A Word for Kinesthetics

Feeling/touching people commonly have trouble deciding which system best fits them. The reason for this is that in our American educational system most instruction has been either by writing things on the board or by talking about them. That is, our culture has favored the seeing and the hearing/speaking people. Most educational experiences, especially in the elementary years, are not "hands on" experiences. As a result, kinesthetics learn to compensate by developing one or both of the other systems. If they *don't* compensate, they usually end up thinking they are dull or slow learners.

Therefore, if you have trouble figuring out which representational system fits you, the likelihood is that you are a kinesthetic and that you have learned to survive in a visual and auditory/tonal world.

Traveling Together with Different Maps

Determining what representational systems the various members of your family use can shed significant light on why you sometimes just can't see eye to eye (or, if you prefer, ear to ear!). Representational systems can cause disharmony and miscommunication because it's hard to travel together when you are using different maps.

The greatest difficulty families experience is when *one family member insists that his or her map is right and the map used by the others is wrong.*

For example, a husband who likes things neat and tidy might constantly fuss at his wife because of her housekeeping habits. He gets irritated when the house is not picked up when he comes home. He's bothered when his wife doesn't clean the crumbs from the back seat of the family car after she's taken the children to the park. More than likely he's a visual.

On the other hand, his wife is a kinesthetic. All that she really cares about is that she and the kids were having fun. In her mind, there are more important things to worry about than keeping everything in place. She thinks her husband's priorities are all mixed up.

Neither is right or wrong. They are just different. Their representational differences affect how they experience their world and, in turn, how they experience their relationship.

A second problem is related to the first. It occurs when *one person discounts or denies that the other person's map is accurate.* Suppose, for example, that a couple agrees to meet for lunch. They both are looking forward to the occasion. However, in communicating about where they will meet, the wife, who is visual, forgets to write down the directions to the restaurant. And the husband, who is auditory/tonal, assumes that because the message was communicated verbally, the meaning was communicated, too. When she finally finds the place, she's thirty minutes late and he's seething with anger.

In the argument that follows each attempts to reconstruct their earlier conversation. She claims that his directions were vague. He claims that she just doesn't listen. What follows involves his attacking her for ignoring him and her attacking him for being insensitive and hostile. Both were acting congruently with their dominant representational system, but each discounts the other's actions, which leads to hurt feelings and conflict.

A third problem occurs when *one person's dominant system is the other person's minimal system.* If one person's dominant system is visual and the other's minimal system is visual, more than likely the couple will have problems. Likewise, if one spouse's dominant system is auditory/tonal and the other's minimal system is auditory/tonal, their problems will be multiplied. Because they experience the world so differently, they can easily find that communication is difficult, if not painful. It can seem as if they are ships passing in the night; they never seem to understand one another.

What a couple like this needs to learn is to communicate in their highest common system. Say the couple above both use their kinesthetic system as a back-up. That will be their highest common system. They will communicate better, therefore, if they learn to communicate with one another in terms of feelings. If they can get away from blaming one another for being different and begin to talk about how they feel, they'll begin to find the common ground they desperately need.

The fourth problem has to do with *whose map causes what problem*. It's common, for example, for visuals and auditory/tonals to insist that what they see or hear determines how they feel. One spouse might say to the other, "How could I not get angry? Just look at the expression on your face." The visual's perception is that what is seen "causes" the feelings of anger. Or an auditory/tonal might say, "If you hadn't yelled at me, my feelings wouldn't have gotten hurt." In this case, the perception is that the dominant auditory/tonal system "causes" the hurt.

Similarly, kinesthetics tend to allow their own feelings to predict what their spouse means to say or interpret how they look. Kinesthetics are prone to being mind readers: "They laughed at me because I was afraid," would be an indication that a person is a kinesthetic and interprets the responses of others based upon his or her internal feelings. Or, "If I tell him I'm angry it will only hurt his feelings and he'll get mad and yell." This person is angry and allows his or her feelings to determine, beforehand, how the other will respond.

Visuals and auditory/tonals tend to blame their feelings on what they see or hear in the other person. Kinesthetics tend to predict what they see or hear based upon what they feel. The answer to the problem is to neither blame nor to predict, but to allow the other person to explain for themselves what they see, hear, or feel. If you don't know, then ask. If they don't know, then tell them.

Learning from Our Differences

If a study of representational systems tells us anything at all, it is that any one system—visual, auditory, or kinesthetic— is just a partial way to experience reality. Personal maps provide a way for finite creatures to make sense of the infinite variety of God's creation.

It would follow that different people with different

representational systems can *complement* each other—not just conflict with one another. Seeing, hearing, and touching people can help each other perceive and understand the richness of God's world.

We think it is significant that, according to Scripture, *Jesus Christ, the Word of God, is knowable by every representational means.* The apostle John wrote in his first Epistle:

> That which was from the beginning, which we have *heard,* which we have *seen with our eyes,* which we have looked upon and *touched with our hands,* concerning the word of life—the life was made manifest, and we saw it, and testify to it, and proclaim to you the eternal life which was with the Father and was made manifest to us (1 John 1:1–2, emphasis added).

We would take this to signify that no one representational system is better or superior to another. In order to experience the fullness of God and his creation, we need each other's unique perspectives. In that light, our differences become a source of enrichment rather than a source of agitation, a source of maturity rather than a source of frustration.

And this brings us back to the basic issue of how we handle our differences. Coping with differences is the bread-and-butter issue of everyday life. It is at the heart of what it means to submit one to another as the apostle Paul encourages us to do in Ephesians 5:21.

Submission, then, according to this line of reasoning, is not only an issue of control or power, but one of acceptance as well. It also becomes a serious indication of what Paul means when he says in 1 Corinthians 13 that "love bears all things." Might not one of the things we must "bear" be the ways we are different from one another?

It is popular to say that we are all created equal but not created the same. Loving one another in spite of, or even because of, our differences is one measure of Christian maturity. It is one goal of real-life marriage.

CHAPTER FIVE

One Flesh,
Yet So Different

"How can we be one when we're so different?"

The question was both fair and appropriate. The phrase from the Book of Genesis, "and the two shall become one flesh," had been a significant part of their wedding vows, and the young woman had taken it seriously. But now she was almost ready to give up.

The young couple sitting in Dennis's office had been married for less than two years. Thus far, the bad times had far outweighed the good ones. Julie's intuition about what was wrong in their marriage had led her to suspect theirs was a case of "irreconcilable differences." But in spite of her suspicions, she was trying to find a way to unravel their problems— if only because of her Christian commitment.

Todd had come to the same conclusion as his wife. But

unlike her, he wasn't willing to try any longer. "We virtually have nothing in common," he commented testily. "Whatever I like to do, she doesn't. And whatever she likes to do, I don't. We're totally opposite from one another. I like to be spontaneous—have fun. But she can't even decide to drive down to the beach and look at the sunset without planning everything out to the itty-bittiest detail.

"And even if I do get her there, she really doesn't enjoy it. She's thinking of the work she has to do back at the apartment. When I say something about it, she gets critical and somehow it all becomes my fault—things would be better if only I would change. I'm sick and tired of her trying to make me over."

Todd's defensiveness echoed in the room—his frustration long ago turned to anger. "Why don't we just call it quits and go our separate ways? Why end up enemies, hating each other? Let's admit we made a mistake and be done with it."

Dennis recognized the pattern. He had seen it many times before. A couple is attracted to one another for a myriad of reasons, only to find that what initially attracted them now repels them.

Julie's question echoes the dilemma almost every couple must face at one time or another: How can two people be one when they're so fundamentally different?

We've already suggested that understanding, accepting, and even appreciating our differences is a fundamental axiom in a real-life marriage. In the previous chapter we showed that sometimes these differences take the form of internal maps or representational systems, which significantly determine how we perceive the world. In this chapter we will focus upon another way in which human beings differ—*temperament*. And then we hope to pinpoint some basic principles which can help a couple achieve unity in spite of their differences.

An understanding of the concept of temperament helps explain the stress and the terrible communication difficulties exhibited between the young couple in Dennis's office. What was taking place in the relationship between Todd and Julie takes place between most couples in real life. Their differences were driving them apart because their temperaments were functionally opposite.

What Is Temperament?

But just what do we mean when we speak of temperament? The concept is centuries old. In fact, the Greek philosopher Hippocrates was the first to define human differences in this light. His four basic categories of sanguine, choleric, phlegmatic, and melancholic have been explored and repeated by others throughout the years, even by recent Christian writers such as Tim LaHaye.

Hippocrates stressed that the differences between people are intrinsic to their very being. Reflecting the world view of his day, he interpreted these differences as being derived from four body fluids: blood, phlegm, yellow bile, and black bile. But while this analysis is clearly flawed in terms of our modern understanding of physiology, his insistence that human differences are innate was accurate. He got us moving in the right direction.

Many centuries later, Carl Jung, the Swiss psychiatrist, added significantly to our understanding of temperament. Jung's view was that temperament is the inward manifestation of a personality "function." In other words, according to Jung, temperament is the inner compass for which a person's outward behavior is the visible result.

Following Jung's lead, we would define *temperament* to be *a multifaceted internal psychological compass which is constantly spinning and turning, seeking to orient each of us to the world within us as well as the world around us.*

According to Carl Jung and others, notably Isabel Briggs Myers and David Keirsey, many marital differences reflect the reality that our inner compasses are pointing in different directions. Not only are we often reading from a different map, as is the case with representational systems, but our whole beings are often pointing in different directions. No wonder we can't understand each other!

According to the Jungian view, temperament can be thought of as having eight dimensions, each operating as points on our psychological compass. Our internal temperament compass looks something like figure 1.

Understanding how and why these points on the compass work has been extremely helpful to us in understanding how to handle differences in marriage. It became central in the process that needed to be worked through between Todd and Julie. And it's been very helpful in our own relationship as well.

The Many Aspects of Temperament

As you can tell by the diagram, certain of these points on the compass are opposite from one another and can only be understood in relationship to one another. One way to think of them is to envision each pair as operating along a continuum. Rarely will someone function totally at one end of the continuum; we tend to fall somewhere in between.

What are these points, what do they mean, and how can you identify where you and your spouse fit? That is what we will be looking at here. And we will be especially interested in those points where married partners find themselves at different points of the continuum and experience tension because of their differences.

In order to orient these issues to real life, we will illustrate each of the functions of temperament with an issue that most married couples face in their relationship: entertaining as a couple. We choose this issue not because it is somehow especially relevant to temperament, but because it is one of those tasks that demands a negotiation of differences. How a couple negotiates these differences can become a metaphor or real-life picture of how they handle all the differences in their relationship.'

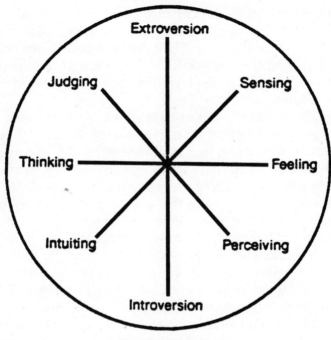

Figure 1
Identifying Your Map

Extroversion vs. Introversion

Extroverts are people who like other people and seem to derive energy from being with them. They are sociable; as far as they're concerned, "the more the merrier." They like visiting with, hanging out with, dropping in on, and being around people. In fact, they need people around in order to feel good. They like parties and they like to socialize. When they entertain they like lots of people. The payoff for them is that being with people charges them up. Being alone drains energy away.

It has been estimated that 75 percent of the people in our culture are extroverts. And because they form the majority, they also determine the norms. It's hard, therefore, for them to understand those at the other end of the continuum.

Introverts, on the other hand, tend to be territorial. They derive energy from being alone, and being with people tends to be hard work for them. They can take crowds for only so long, and then they've got to find solitude. If they must be around people a lot of the time, they find themselves drained and run down.

If 75 percent of people in our culture are extroverts, then the remaining 25 percent are introverts. Because they are forever in the minority, they easily feel out of step and inferior. They're embarrassed that they're less social. Why? Because in an extroverted world, gregariousness is seen as good. Solitude is not. Probably because of this one simple fact, many introverts suffer with varying degrees of low self-esteem. Because they're not as comfortable around people as are extroverts, they feel something's wrong with them.

The marital tension between extroverts and introverts will involve issues of being sociable and being territorial. Conflict arises over issues such as how often to entertain, how many to invite, and what to do after they arrive. To the extrovert, the more the merrier. The introvert, if he or she agrees to entertain at all, will prefer a small gathering of close friends—and will probably be exhausted at the end of the evening.

Vacations can be a problem for an extrovert/introvert couple. The extrovert may revel in spending one or two days among the crowds at Disneyland (to the children's endless delight) only to find that the introverted spouse is dragging his or her feet. For the introvert, an ideal vacation is camping on a secluded beach or even puttering around the house. And no matter where the family goes, the fewer people around, the better.

The extroversion/introversion difference is common among marriages because probably at no other points on the compass do opposites attract as much as between extroverts and introverts.

To get an idea where you and your spouse are on the extrovert/introvert continuum, turn to the first chart in figure

2—the one labeled "Extroversion vs. Introversion." The chart is made up of eight pairs of words or phrases with numbers on a continuum between them. For each pair of words or phrases, select the number that you think describes where you fit on the continuum. Circle that number.

Make yourself make a choice for each pair. If neither seems to apply, try to go with your "gut reaction"; choose the one that sounds more appealing to you. Or ask someone who knows you well to help you decide.

When you are finished with the chart, add up the individual total for each side. If the higher number is on the extroverted side, write an **E** in the blank that says "Result." Write an **I** if the number is higher on the introverted side. If the numbers on either side are the same, write an **X** rather than an **E** or an **I**.

Sensing vs. Intuiting

The next set of opposites has to do with qualities Jung called "sensation" and "intuition."

Sensing people think of themselves as practical and tangible. The word that best describes them is "sensible." They value experience, both past and present. As far as they're concerned, what the world needs are more people who are dealing with reality (as they define it). They are "no-nonsense" kind of people. The old line from the TV program, "Dragnet," fits their view of the world: "Just the facts, ma'am." They also tend to be "hands-on" people. By this we mean that they prefer to get involved in the doing of a project in order to understand it. They tend to enjoy details because they can get a better handle on the issues if the details are known. They resist change, until they fully understand *how* it will justify the effort and *how* it will be implemented step by step.

Jung suggested that sensing types, if they were farmers, would plant one crop, harvest it, count their money, and then plan for the next crop. They like to stay with a task until it's done and become agitated with those who don't.

Extroversion vs. Introversion

Extroversion		Introversion
sociable	5 4 3 2 1 1 2 3 4 5	territorial
likes interaction	5 4 3 2 1 1 2 3 4 5	likes solitude
externally oriented	5 4 3 2 1 1 2 3 4 5	internally oriented
extensive relationships	5 4 3 2 1 1 2 3 4 5	intensive relationships
many relationships	5 4 3 2 1 1 2 3 4 5	few relationships
expends energy	5 4 3 2 1 1 2 3 4 5	conserves energy
prefers company	5 4 3 2 1 1 2 3 4 5	prefers solitude

Total Extroversion Score _____   Total Introversion Score _____

Result _____ (letter)

Sensing vs. Intuiting

Sensing		INtuiting
trusts experience	5 4 3 2 1 1 2 3 4 5	trusts hunches
past/present oriented	5 4 3 2 1 1 2 3 4 5	future oriented
reality based	5 4 3 2 1 1 2 3 4 5	speculative
perspiration	5 4 3 2 1 1 2 3 4 5	inspiration
actualities	5 4 3 2 1 1 2 3 4 5	possibilities
likes facts	5 4 3 2 1 1 2 3 4 5	likes ideas
what works	5 4 3 2 1 1 2 3 4 5	what can be

Total Sensing Score _____   Total INtuiting Score _____

Result _____ (letter)

Figure 2:

Thinking vs. Feeling

Thinking		Feeling
objective	5 4 3 2 1 1 2 3 4 5	subjective
impersonal	5 4 3 2 1 1 2 3 4 5	personal
analysis of facts	5 4 3 2 1 1 2 3 4 5	analysis of relationships
reason	5 4 3 2 1 1 2 3 4 5	emotion
concern for justice	5 4 3 2 1 1 2 3 4 5	concern for harmony
cares most about principles	5 4 3 2 1 1 2 3 4 5	cares most about personalities
loves facts	5 4 3 2 1 1 2 3 4 5	loves stories
Total Thinking Score_____		Total Feeling Score_____

Result _____ (letter)

Judging vs. Perceiving

Judging		Perceiving
firm	5 4 3 2 1 1 2 3 4 5	flexible
decides now	5 4 3 2 1 1 2 3 4 5	waits
plans	5 4 3 2 1 1 2 3 4 5	adapts
"pin it down"	5 4 3 2 1 1 2 3 4 5	"let it happen"
organizes others	5 4 3 2 1 1 2 3 4 5	leaves them alone
makes decisions	5 4 3 2 1 1 2 3 4 5	keeps options open
"work now, play later"	5 4 3 2 1 1 2 3 4 5	"play now, work later"
Total Judging Score_____		Total Perceiving Score_____

Result _____ (letter)

Discovering Your Temperament

It's been estimated that 75 percent of the people in this culture are sensing types. Thus, like the extroverts, they form the majority and establish the norms. It's hard for them to understand their opposites.

Intuiting people love possibilities. They are likely to go with their hunches—which most often turn out to be right. They like to daydream and fantasize—and everything else that goes with anticipating the future. Thus, they are very creative. When they plan, they tend to think in terms of the whole, rather than just the parts; as far as they are concerned, someone else can take care of the details. The future usually appeals to them more than the past and the present. They are visionaries. They usually bring insight and creative energy to their relationships.

If they were farmers, their tendency would be to plant a crop and then to go off to some other project, leaving the harvest and the counting of the profit or loss to someone else. They like to skip around, and they tend to become bored if they stay in one place too long. They often embrace change.

The marital tension between sensing and intuiting types is between practicalities and possibilities. If 75 percent of the population is sensing in its orientation, 25 percent is intuiting. Those who have analyzed in depth this difference are of the opinion that it is the greatest source of miscommunication and misunderstanding between people in general and couples in particular. It is the conflict between concrete and abstract, between hunches and facts, between possibilities and actualities.

When it comes to the issue of entertaining, sensing types enjoy the down-to-earth reality of the moment and the details of doing what needs to be done. What matters is what *is*—in the here and now—not what will be.

To determine where you each fit in the sensing/intuiting continuum, use the second chart in figure 2—the one labeled "Sensing vs. Intuiting." Just as you did on the extrovert/introvert chart, circle a number describing where you fall on the continuum between each pair of words. Total up the numbers on each side and determine the result according to which side has the higher number. Designate your result with an **S** if you're a sensing type and an **N** if you're an intuiting type. (The **I** has already been used to designate introverts.) And write down an **X** if you're right in the middle.

Thinking vs. Feeling

Thinking types pride themselves on being objective and logical. They tilt toward reason and justice when making a decision or evaluating an issue. Because of their love of information, facts, and logic, they sometimes get a reputation for being impersonal rather than personal.

Feeling types, on the other hand, pride themselves on being personal rather than impersonal. They tend to be emotional and subjective and tilt toward passion and mercy when it comes to making a decision or evaluating an issue. They focus on the "human" elements of a situation.

The marital tension between thinking and feeling types revolves around the issues of the impersonal and the personal, reason and emotion. Estimates are that the population splits about 50/50 when it comes to percentages for these types. However, it is the only dimension on the temperament compass that is gender-specific, with men being approximately 60 percent thinking and women 60 percent feeling in their orientation.

When it comes to hospitality, the thinking person (male or female), probably will not be as open to the idea as will the feeling type unless it fits into some predetermined plan. He or she sees no point in entertaining unless there's a "reason" for it.

If thinking types do entertain, they tend to think in terms of: "How much is it going to cost?" or "Do we have enough of this or enough of that?" The practicalities of the evening may cause them to scale down their plans. They tend to get caught up in the details: "What's the schedule in terms of when the guests are coming, and when are they leaving?" If it gets too late, thinking people can be blunt and direct. "The party's over. Good night, folks. Tomorrow's another day."

Feeling types, on the other hand, become involved with the people who are there, sometimes forgetting the practicalities involved. It's not unusual for feeling types to get lost in a conversation or to get involved with someone's story and to forget to fill the punch bowl or pick up the dishes after dinner. Their feeling is that things can wait; people can't.

To determine where you are on this continuum, fill out the third chart in figure 2, following the procedure you used for the two previous charts. Designate your result with a **T** for thinking and an **F** for feeling.

Judging vs. Perceiving

The fourth pair of characteristics which forms the basis of temperament is judging/perceiving. Unfortunately, in this case, Jung's terminology can be misleading, for we are not really talking about making "judgments" in the sense of decisions or pronouncements.

In this specialized sense, judging has to do with the need to have "closure" in life, to have things settled and tied down, with no loose ends. Judging types love—even need—deadlines. They like lists and the organization which lists bring. It's tough on them to have jobs undone, plans not made or finished, and decisions left hanging.

In addition to having this strong need for closure, judging people tend to function out of a sense of duty. To them, work comes before play and play comes only after everything else is done. Therefore, judging types easily become weary and fatigued. Rest, seen as a form of play, comes last, if at all.

Perceiving types, on the other hand, can be characterized by the word *pending*. They hate to be tied down and will often change their minds just for the fun of it. They sometimes procrastinate because of this need to keep things open-ended, not because they don't want to get the work done. For them, deadlines are like strait jackets. In addition to having an open-ended approach toward life, perceiving types tend to like to play before they work. If work can be put off until after play, they'll do it.

The marital tension between judging and perceiving types has to do with these needs to have closure or to leave things open-ended. It also has to do with the outlook toward toward work and play. Each partner tends to want to order their life together according to opposite priorities.

In terms of hospitality in the home, judging types like to have plans made and pinned down. Not knowing what's going to happen is hard on them. Perceiving types are just the opposite. Their idea of a great evening is one when they just "let things happen." In their view, planning destroys the spontaneity. The "work before play" versus "play before work" tension with their spouse can easily destroy their motivation to entertain at all—especially if they see it as something they "should" do. Often they think it's easier to forget the whole thing and do nothing at all.

To decide which type you are, fill in the final chart in figure 2—"Judging vs. Perceiving." Write a **J** in the results blank if your judging score is higher or a **P** if your perceiving score is higher.

The Algebra of Marriage

If you completed the work on the four charts in figure 2, you now have a composite pattern consisting of four letters: **E** or **I**, **S** or **N**, **T** or **F**, and **J** or **P**. These characteristics operate together to form your temperament or internal compass. Keirsey and Bates in their book, *Please Understand Me*, identify four major temperament combinations: **SP**, **SJ**, **NT**, or **NF**. Since we are writing a book about marriage, we'll now look at the most frequently occurring combinations and what happens when people displaying these temperament combinations marry one another.

The first major combination is the **SP** or *free spirit*.

Wherever the wind blows is where the SP is likely to be. They are spontaneous and very much into the experience of the moment. To them, whatever sets them free is good; whatever ties them down isn't. They love sex and enjoy both giving and receiving pleasure. In fact, sometimes it appears that their whole life is spent pursuing these ends. They're not known for moderation; for them it's all or nothing. Their carefree approach toward life makes them an exciting prospect to marry but a tough person to stay married to. Often they struggle with commitment.

The second major combination is the **SJ** or *faithful partner.* The SJs are known for their orientation toward duty and service to others. They live as if life were filled with an endless chain of obligations, each to be met and fulfilled and each to be replaced by another. They can be in charge or they can follow— whatever needs to be done to get the task accomplished.

SJs are hard workers and find it hard to tolerate those who aren't. Sometimes their spouses accuse them of being plodders, putting one foot down in front of the other, without "smelling the roses" as they go through life. But in terms of the realities of marriage, they get things done. They believe in God and country, motherhood and apple pie, and easily become irritated with those whose attitudes toward life are less solemn. They have absolutely no problem with commitment at all.

The third major combination is the **NT** or *Field Marshal.* NTs are into control; they are usually in charge. Their thinking, combined with their intuitive sense, allows them to think things through logically while at the same time seeing things that others don't. Sometimes they can be aloof and removed from the details of a marriage. They can be sparing with their affection and seem self-sufficient, and they become easily irritated with those who aren't. They can be manipulative and are accustomed to getting their own way.

The fourth, and last, major combination of temperament styles is the **NF** or *romantic courtier.* NFs are by nature romantic and charming. They can be warm, affectionate, and supportive. They can also be fickle and restless if their relationships become conflict plagued and/or mundane. Their strength—intuition coupled with feeling—makes them aware of what's going on around them while at the same time impatient with those who aren't. They love a "cause" and will commit themselves to it. They are good with people individually or in groups.

Each combination has its strengths and its potential weaknesses. Each brings a unique perspective to the relationship.

For the **SP** the most important thing is freedom and experience, for the **SJ** it's work and duty, for the **NT** it's analysis and control, and for the **NF** it's romance and vision. None of these characteristics is either good or bad in and of itself. But when one comes up against its opposite, sparks can fly!

You'll remember that this chapter began with the story of a couple who came to Dennis's office for counseling. In that couple, Todd was an SP and Julie was an SJ. Their marriage was in conflict because of the tension between his emphasis on freedom and her stress on duty, his need for pleasure and her drive to work.

Todd and Julie had never faced up to the reason they married each other, which was that they each chose someone with a characteristic they instinctively knew they lacked. And each had also never faced up to what it meant to be in a real-life, day-to-day relationship with a person who was fundamentally different. These issues of understanding and facing their differences were at the heart of the work before them.

Solving the Equation

Because temperament is such a basic part of our being, it can easily color our perception of our marriages to such an extent that we fail to see and appreciate the positive implications of our differences. It is at times like these that we need to look to God rather than to our own experience for our guidance.

In facing our temperamental differences, the two of us have come to rely heavily on two verses of scripture found in Paul's letter to the Philippians.

> Do nothing out of selfish ambition or vain conceit, but in humility consider others better than yourselves. Each of you should look not only to your own interests, but also to the interests of others (Phil. 2:3–4, NIV).

Three principles have emerged from these verses that have helped us and others cope with our differences in temperament. They represent the ways in which our faith and our temperaments have intersected in terms of scripture. We share them as a means of provoking a dialogue for you. Think about them and talk about them.

In terms of our marriage, Lucy is an ENFJ, and Dennis is an INFP. As you can see, our major differences are between Lucy's E and Dennis's I, and Lucy's J and Dennis's P.

Concerning the first difference, Lucy is very much a social being. In particular, she loves to entertain. She's a "more the merrier" kind of person. Dennis is less so. Early on in our marriage, how often we would entertain and how many people we would invite were very real points of tension between us, points that had to be negotiated on almost a daily basis. On the whole, our marriage today is more E than it is I. Dennis has evolved into more of an extrovert; he has learned to adapt to Lucy's needs.

In contrast, our differences in terms of J and P have tilted more in Dennis's direction. Early on, Lucy needed everything to be planned out. Dennis was more "hang loose." As a result of these differences, there were times that one could cut the tension between us with a knife.

Fortunately for us, in the major combinations of temperaments, we are both NF's, the romantic courtier. We both like a challenge and can easily be caught up in the romance of an idea or moment. The difficulty for us comes when we need to plan ahead or think things through. At those times, it would be useful if one or the other of us would be more of an NT.

The bottom line is that we are more alike than we are different, and the ways in which we are different establish the areas in which we need to be sensitive and flexible.

But in a real life marriage, people change when they can and accept things when they can't. Looking back, each of us has adapted to the other and for the most part, it's been a two-way street. The principles that follow have been helpful in our pilgrimage.

The first principle is that *to serve one another is more important than the need to be right or the need to control the relationship.* Paul writes to the Philippians and exhorts them to avoid "selfish ambition" and "vain conceit." Clearly there's enough of both of these in any relationship to create distance and turn basic differences into marital discord.

Whether it's differences in representational systems or in temperament, sufficient grounds exist to insist on one's own way.

Paul's advice is to take the higher ground. Selfishness says that our way is right and the other person is wrong. Conceit interprets that selfishness in such a way as to legitimize our point of view and make the other person the bad guy.

The viewpoint of the servant, on the other hand, is to preserve the dignity of the other person through the recognition that how that person perceives and responds to the world is right and good to him or her. The other person's perception needs to be acknowledged and respected, even adapted to. "Love doesn't seek its own way" is another way of saying the same thing.

The second principle is that *it's important to assert your own point of view even when it's different, and even if it's ignored.* Paul says that we should "look *not only* to [our] own interests, but also to the interests of others."

The "not only" in that verse implies a key point that is often overlooked. Paul is assuming that his readers possess sufficient ego strength to assert their desires and their wishes. Some partners in a marriage have never said openly and out loud what it is that they want or how it is they differ. And so it is little wonder that they feel their wants and needs are being overlooked.

The third principle is that *healthy relationships are implicitly fair and even—but not necessarily equal. Unhealthy relationships are unfair and uneven.* Another implication of that "not only" in Philippians 2 is the idea of evenness or balance between two people.

The emphasis in our recent history as a culture has been upon radical equality, not balance—we think that everything must be exactly equal in order to be good and right.

But our interpretation of what Paul is saying is that what is equitable is ultimately more important than what is equal. Real life is seldom equal, but it can be fair and equitable. Said in another way, marital unity does not mean sameness. Becoming one is not the same as being alike.

Here's the challenge we all must face: maintaining unity in the face of differences. And it seems to us that a lesson from John 17:20–23 is relevant here. Jesus prayed in his great, high-priestly prayer that Christians would be one, even as he and the Father are one. Clearly, he didn't mean that all Christians should be identical! Oneness is different from sameness. And that is true for marriage, just as it is for the Christian family.

Though our differences necessarily separate us in terms of how we perceive the world around us and how we orient ourselves to life, they need not destroy the unity of a relationship. In fact, as we have indicated earlier, our differences may even enhance our unity by complementing each other— making the whole greater than the sum of the parts.

Our prayer for you, then, is that understanding the various ways you are different from each other can help you learn to be one, just as your Creator intended you to be from the beginning.

CHAPTER SIX

Solving the Dual-Career Puzzle

Often couples focus on different things in recalling their history together. For one couple, the memories center around the various houses they've lived in. Another couple remembers where one or more of their children were born. Still another focuses upon vivid events or crises. Some key event or thing is used to bind the past to the present and to frame the future.

As we were remembering the events in our life that provide the backdrop for this chapter, the most vivid memory that surfaced for us had to do with Lucy's decision to reenter the work force and Dennis's reaction to it.

Lucy has worked outside the home for most of our marriage. Before the children were born, she worked full time while Dennis finished his undergraduate degree in college.

Then, throughout our five years in seminary, she worked part time as a faculty secretary, taking time off only to have two babies, and returning to the job as soon as the babies were a bit older.

The next five years, Lucy's time was spent supporting Dennis in his ministry as an associate pastor in a large church and developing a ministry of her own among the young women of the church, as she and they attempted to cope with the realities of rearing young families.

After eleven years of marriage, Dennis moved from ministry in the local church to ministry in a parachurch organization, of which he had been appointed executive director. Lucy settled in making a home for the family and, once again, forging a ministry among the women in our new church home. Dennis, who was busy finishing his Ph.D. in Marriage and Family at USC and working full time to support the family, simply assumed that all was well with Lucy.

But Lucy was bored! Our youngest child, Shannon, had entered school, and Lucy had long ago mastered the skills of homemaking. She was restless; she needed a new challenge. And so she decided that she would return to the job market.

But when Lucy approached Dennis with the idea, his response blew her away: "I don't think I want you working. We need you at home."

The conversation took place in the front seat of the car as we were driving home from one of Dennis's speaking engagements. The ride was filled with tension, which soon escalated and erupted into a full-scale argument. And then it went from a full-scale argument to a destructive quarrel!

Dennis's voice filled the car with anger: "I said no, and I don't want to talk about it anymore!"

What had begun as a discussion concerning Lucy's work deteriorated into an issue of authority. According to the pattern we had lived for the first decade of our marriage, Dennis always had the final word. And he intended for this argument to end the same way.

Up until that point we had lived a traditional "Christian"

marriage, assuming that authority in a relationship rested with the male and that in marriage it rested with the husband. Dennis's training in seminary had reinforced this belief, and Lucy had acquiesced willingly. After all, he was the "head" of the household, wasn't he?

And so Lucy's response to Dennis's ultimatum completely surprised and befuddled Dennis. She buried her face in her hands and began to cry, rocking back and forth in obvious emotional agony.

"You can't treat me this way. I'm a person. I'm a person. I'm a person. I'm a person."

The intensity of her pain shocked us both. Clearly, something was desperately wrong. But we weren't exactly sure what!

We arrived home and stumbled from the car into the house. The distance between us that night seemed as great as at any time in our thirteen years of marriage. We went to sleep deeply troubled by the quarrel, yet unable to fathom why the hurt was so deep.

The Question of Power

Looking back on that incident, we can now see more clearly what was baffling to us then. There were really two issues involved. The surface issue had to do with Lucy's desire to work outside the home again, as she had on and off for years.

But the deeper issue had to do with power in our marriage. Our interaction had demonstrated that the effective power in our relationship rested with Dennis. Lucy's feelings of being a "nonperson" were the result of her powerlessness.

Now, in every relationship, the issue of power operates simultaneously at three levels. The first has to do with *who does what*—in our case, who was to work where and why. Our assumption at that point was that we shared power in this area. We both worked equally and fairly in the support of the family.

But at the second level the balance of power in our relationship became clearer. This level has to do with *who decides who does what*. This is where the power shifted completely toward Dennis's side of the ledger. He was making the decisions, and his decision was that Lucy was to work in the home.

The third level has to do with *who decides how the rules about decision making are to be interpreted and/or changed*. Again, at this third level the power was completely Dennis's.

Our quarrel in the front seat of the car, however, changed things forever for us as far as power was concerned. Never before had Dennis realized that his power was so absolute and that Lucy could be so unhappy as a result.

Dennis was forced to evaluate both why he had been so adamant and what was really wrong in the relationship.

The answer to why he was so adamant had to do with his insecurity. He had to face the fact that part of the reason he didn't want Lucy working out in the "real" world had to do with his fears about his performance as a husband and father. Suppose she went to work in an office and found someone else more supportive and attractive. As busy as he was trying to finish his degree and make a living, he felt he wasn't doing a very good job at being an attentive husband, and he felt threatened.

The answer to what was really wrong in our relationship had to do with the distribution of power. Dennis had it all, and he had never faced what that meant.

Subsequently, his study of the scriptures led him to realize that his interpretation of the New Testament passages having to do with husband-and-wife relationships (especially Ephesians 5, which is often cited as the "standard" for Christian marriage), had been distorted by his chauvinistic point of view, which in turn was based on both his upbringing and his convenience.

The liberating key for Dennis was the scriptural emphasis upon *mutual submission rather than unilateral submission*. Husbands and wives are to submit to one another, rather than only one to the other. This was the radical teaching of the apostle Paul. It has become a central concept in the understanding of our own relationship.

Applied to the issue of power in the relationship, this concept meant that not only were both of us to share in the work of the marriage; we both were to share in making the *decisions* about who does the work. And we were to decide together about how we would decide.

In practical terms, it meant that whether Lucy went back to work or not had to be a mutual decision. It also meant that Dennis couldn't decide for her, nor could he change the rules about making the decision.

The results of really applying Paul's principle of mutual submission to our marriage have been revolutionary. Since that day, our relationship has never been the same. Frankly, it's been much more complicated; things were easier when one person controlled the relationship. But we both agree that sharing the responsibility has made our relationship better.

Lucy did go back to work at that time, and we both agreed that it was the right choice. And Dennis did have to deal with his insecurities and decide he was willing to trust her with the temptations of real life.

Later, we decided together that Lucy would quit her job, return to school, and finish her undergraduate degree. She has since finished her master's degree as well and is now ensconced in a satisfying career of her own. We are a dual-career couple and proud of it.

We began the chapter with this rather lengthy illustration because we believe that working through the issues of power is a primary need for any marriage relationship—and especially for dual-career couples. Unless husbands and wives come to some arrangement of shared responsibility for the work and the choices of life, marriage is bound to be fraught with problems.

We believe, of course, that the issues of power and mutual submission are relevant to any real-life marriage, whether a couple is dual career or not. But when both partners work outside the home, the issues become more complex, and the complexity needs to be evaluated and faced realistically.

The Dilemmas of a Dual-Career Couple

Several major studies of dual-career marriages have surfaced in the recent past, and one of the most significant is the work of Dr. Uma Sekaran, Professor of Management at Southern Illinois University. In her 1986 book, *Dual Career Families,* Dr. Sekaran lists five dilemmas or points of tension faced by most dual-career couples. These dilemmas (Note how often this word surfaces when we talk about marriage in the real world!) provide us with an astute analysis of the pieces of the dual-career puzzle.

The dilemmas pinpointed by Dr. Sekaran are (1) role overload, (2) identity issues, (3) role-cycling, (4) social network issues, and (5) normative sanctions. The labels are technical. The issues are not. We'll explain each one and then discuss what can be done about it.

Dr. Sekaran calls the first dilemma *role overload.* This has to do with the real-life fact that *there are more hats to wear than there are hours in the day.* As a couple attends to the demands of home and children before and after a busy day at work, strain and fatigue are commonplace. This is true especially for women because they tend to take on a greater proportion of the burdens of child care and homemaking. The troublesome question becomes, "What's a mother to do?"

The second dilemma, *role or identity confusion,* has to do with the fear that *you cannot succeed both at work and at home.* You must choose one or the other.

For example, a husband wno chooses to be more active in the home may begin to doubt his "manliness." Or a wife might agonize over whether she can possibly be a "good" mother if a major part of her energy and waking time is spent away from home. What a terrible bind to be caught in—thinking you cannot be both "good" at work and "good" at home.

Role-cycling, the third dilemma, concerns *when, how many, and how often to have children.*

If a couple waits too long to have children, the wife risks health complications for herself and/or the children. But if they begin early, she risks getting behind in her career and never "catching up."

The *social network* dilemma has to do with the fact that *more work means less time for friends and family.* Dual-career couples have significantly less discretionary time and energy. It's virtually impossible to just "get together sometime." In order to cope, they must deliberately cultivate friendships, tightly scheduling them on an already overcrowded calendar. And in so doing they run the risk of offending those who think that friendship should be "spontaneous" or that it's demeaning to "make an appointment" to see a friend.

The dilemma of *normative sanctions* has to do with *fitting in and keeping up.* By definition, dual-career couples are nontraditional. This is hard on some people, perhaps especially Christians, who have historically espoused the "traditional" family model.

According to the popular notion, traditional couples have children. Dual-career couples may choose not to. That's tough on potential grandparents. If the dual-career couple does have children, they may be too busy at times to make it to open house or parent conferences at school. That's tough on kids. These couples usually try to do it all. That's hard on Mom and Dad.

As you can see, the choice to pursue two careers creates many complexities. It's especially tough on the woman because, according to research, she's the one who is usually expected to adapt. The assumption in broader society as well as in the church is that her "place" is in the home—or at least that she doesn't have the right to work outside the home unless she also does a great job at home. The typical solution is for her to try to be a "superwife" and "supermother." The problem is that, practically speaking, very few of us are "superpeople" and that's what it takes to be successful. The task of maintaining a dual-career marriage is tough. It can be done, but it takes two—both a wife and a husband—to make it work.

Challenging Some Assumptions

Before we make suggestions as to what can be done about the complex issues of a dual-career marriage, several assumptions need to be challenged. These assumptions form the background to the dual-career puzzle, which in turn influences the choices we make and the stress and tension we feel.

What are those assumptions? A lot of them concern traditional ideas about the role of women in the world and especially in the home.

It is our opinion, for instance, that much of the teaching in the church about the woman's role is based upon a Victorian cultural standard rather than upon the scriptures or even historical reality.

The cultural myth has at least two components. The first has to do with where men and women work. According to the myth, women work in the home and men work outside the home. But the difficulty here is that women have *always* worked outside the home as well as in the home. The traditional roles of women throughout human history have involved gathering food, carrying water, and other "outside" (if domestic) chores. Or, as is also the case with many contemporary women, they have worked in commercial enterprises. Perhaps the greatest example of this commercial and entrepreneurial activity is the woman of Proverbs 31:10–31.

But other women in Scripture worked side by side with their husbands as well. Priscilla and Aquilla in the Book of Acts shared work, responsibility, ministry, and even risk and danger (see Rom. 16:3–4).

Women have always worked outside of the home. They

do in our culture today, and they do in most of the cultures of the world, especially those in the underdeveloped world. Throughout history, the norm has been for both spouses to work outside the home in order to sustain the family.

The rub, then, is not who works outside the home—but who does what work *inside* the home—and it's usually the woman.

The second part of the traditional myth about women's roles involves the notion that there is an intrinsic gratification that goes along with being a wife and mother—a gratification that is not there for the roles of husband and father. The assumption is that every woman ought to be fulfilled and happy solely in and through the roles of wife and mother. The reality is not that clear and convenient, however.

In the midst of our discussions about whether or not Lucy would develop a career of her own, Dennis came to realize that there was a lot more to who *he* was as a person than his roles as husband and father. And yet he thought Lucy should be fulfilled as a person solely through her domestic identity!

Now, we definitely are not trying to say that homemaking and parenting are inferior or demeaning. These roles are significant and important, and for many people they are a high calling. But for many people these roles are limiting. They were for Dennis. Why not for Lucy?

After our argument in the car, for Dennis to continue defining our relationship as we had always defined it would have been the height of arrogance. But simply facing the inconsistencies of that logic provoked a change in the relationship.

What was needed was a commitment on both of our parts to the belief that *each of us needed the freedom to reach our potential for God, as we mutually decided what that potential would be—and always under the guidance and authority of Scripture.* We recommend that commitment to you—dual-career couple or not.

What we are arguing for is that a couple mutually decide what they want their lives to be rather than having one partner do the deciding. A couple may well decide that the woman will be a full-time homemaker. If that is their choice, she should be able to do so without feeling ashamed because she is choosing something less in terms of a vocation. If she decides to work outside the home, that's well and good, too.

The greater issue, in our opinion, has to do with each person's fulfilling their potential as human beings created in the image of God.

Another assumption we think must be challenged has to do with certain home tasks arbitrarily being assigned to the male or female partner.

For example, if the marital and parental tasks are assigned primarily to the wife, it frees the husband to choose only those tasks in the home that he wants and to ignore those he doesn't. The scales of responsibility for the marriage and the family easily tilt that way, and the result is often that she becomes disgruntled at best and resentful and angry at worst.

Real-life marriage is rife with examples.

Take, for instance, the matter of changing diapers. Some men think of themselves as being liberated if they're willing to change the baby's diapers when they're wet but not when they're soiled. According to Erma Bombeck, however, nowhere does it say that a man's hands will fall off if he touches dirty diapers. If the roles are fixed according to gender, the male is free to pick and choose as to what parenting tasks he will undertake.

But the opposite is true as well. Take the matter of financial responsibility. Nowhere does it say that women use credit cards and men pay the bills. But we both know of couples whose marriages have been strained to the breaking point over just this issue—the wife spends and the husband coughs up the cash.

Some Practical Principles

What can be done? Here are some things that we've tried or that we know have been successful in other relationships.

We're obviously not experts, although we probably are veterans. We share them out of our belief that most couples need only to broach the subject of their relationship seriously in order for there to be change. We ask that you think about these principles. Talk about them, and then decide for yourselves about incorporating them in your marriage.

Our first principle has to do with role flexibility, and it evolved in the arena of real life. It is that *whoever can do a household task does it.* Practically speaking, in our home this principle takes the form of "the last one out makes the bed." Even after Lucy began working, making the bed was considered to be her job, even if she was up before Dennis and he was the last one out. You can imagine the times that frustration occurred simply because we assumed that some things are just "women's work" (or "a man's job"). For a dual-career couple, household chores must be shared in order for there to be any sense of fairness in the relationship.

Think about it. Very few tasks are really gender-specific. Most things around the home can be done by either spouse— other than having babies, of course.

Our second principle is that *if you insist on setting the standards by yourself, you'll probably end up doing the job by yourself.* This logic is the genius behind theories of participatory management. This is a general principle, of course. You obviously don't let a five-year-old determine the absolute standards of cleanliness for his or her room. If you did, the only winners would be the roaches. What is at stake, however, is the need for those who do the work to be responsible for their performance and to have a say in establishing the standard of performance.

The third principle is related to the second. It is that *you can't expect rookies to perform at the level of veterans.* One of the greatest disincentives in a family is for the pro to criticize the work of the beginner. This applies to cooking, gardening— any task. Sometimes the person who has become skilled at a task must lessen his or her demands in order for learning to take place and tasks to be shared more equally.

These last two principles have been especially hard on Lucy. She wants the house clean, but doesn't want to accept what "clean" means to the others in the house who do the work. When this happens, the issue quickly becomes one of power and control. She's had to become more flexible than before. And she's still working on it.

The fourth principle has to do with taking responsibility for a task. The principle is that *helping is often not enough.*

Years ago, Lucy's decision to go back to school meant her taking classes late in the afternoon. It also meant that Dennis was responsible for the evening meal on the night she was late. One evening she came home to find nothing done.

"What's for dinner?" she asked.

"I don't know," he replied. "You didn't put anything out to fix, so I didn't start."

After several heated words, it became obvious to us both that we had been operating as if cooking the meals were really Lucy's job and that Dennis was only her "helper." If the "helpee" didn't plan or initiate the meal, then the "helper" didn't get it done.

That attitude needed renegotiating. "Helping" just wasn't enough; Dennis had to buy into the ultimate responsibility. If you're a dual-career couple, the responsibility must be shared, as well as the work.

The fifth principle is that *you can only do what you can do. You can't do more, so don't try, and don't feel guilty.* This is our answer to the Excedrin® headache. And again, this is toughest for Lucy. She habitually thinks she has to do everything, even when it's impossible.

It's hard accepting the limitations two careers place on your time and energy. However, if you don't accept realistic limitations, you can drive yourself into the ground—and that's not good for anyone.

Our sixth principle has to do with friends and family. It is that *if there have to be fewer people in your life, make the relationships better.* Good friends and close family are hard to come by. If the two of you work outside the home, the circumference of your social world will of necessity be smaller. But you can learn to focus on those times you're with the ones who are important to you and make the most of them.

Over the long haul, those who understand your lifestyle will provide the support you need. Probably they need, or will need, the same from you.

The last principle of all is *learn to play, so that you'll like your work*. This has to do with leisure and the place it has in the re-creation of your soul and spirit.

In our family, this principle is hardest for Dennis to follow. Over the years, we've gotten into the habit of taking "busman's holidays"; that is, we try to vacation while Dennis is speaking at a conference. But this just doesn't work as a long-term solution. Everyone needs a time or an activity that is unrelated to his or her work. Research shows that those who have a life outside of their work have a life that is ultimately more productive and satisfying. Even God rested on the seventh day.

A final word about this chapter. It is a fact that two income families are now in the majority and many of these families involve dual careers. However, this is the first generation in which it is socially appropriate for both the woman and the man to have goals of their own. You are pioneers.

As you think through your journey, be open to God's spirit to lead you to formulate the principles that help you most. And most of all, be willing to learn as you go.

CHAPTER SEVEN

The Dilemma of the Double-Minded

An old French proverb states, "You must not only want what you want. You must want what your wants lead to."

In terms of real-life marriage, this proverb strikes a very basic chord. It hints at a basic truth of human relationships: Like it or not, whatever we sow, we reap. Every culture seems to have a saying like that which casts responsibility for life onto the shoulders of the one who is living it. That's not a very comforting thought, but it's true nonetheless.

This chapter and the next are about values and their impact upon real-life marriage. It's a difficult subject both in the writing and in the reading. Little else is as disconcerting as looking hard at why we do what we do. In thinking, talking, and writing about the subject, we found ourselves squirming under the weight of the words.

We are who we are, and we do what we do, because we want it that way. It's that simple. In the end, there's no one else to blame for ourselves but ourselves!

Perhaps it's not true in your marriage, but it certainly is in ours: each of us routinely blames the other for our own circumstances. We seem to take turns—first, one is the persecutor and the other is the victim, then vice versa.

Whether it's an issue as big as money or as small as who's responsible for taking the wrong direction in the car, the pattern is to put the blame on the other person. So many fights occur because one or the other of us doesn't want to take responsibility for the problem—whatever the problem is—and to admit that at the root of the problem may be something as basic as our own individual value system.

Lucy's grandmother had another way of looking at the issue. She often said in her later years, "The older we get, the more we become what we really are." What we took her to mean was that as she became older she didn't have the energy to play the psychological or relational games she had played when she was younger. Therefore, if you didn't want to take her the way she really was, then that was your problem. She was tired of pretending to be what people expected of her.

There's a terribly important message in both the French proverb and in Grandma's wisdom. *When it comes to real people in real marriages, over time we become who we really are; and who we really are is who we want to be.*

The Congruence between Faith and Works

In the New Testament, James asserts that there is a necessary relationship between what we believe and how we live— between our faith and our works (James 2:14–20). According to James, our faith in God demands congruence with how we treat our neighbor. When we try to separate faith and works, we become what James calls "double-minded." We simply can't live out God's values and the world's values at the same time.

What we'd like to suggest is that the same argument holds true in other significant relationships as well. In fact, how we treat one another in our marriages is probably a better mirror of our relationship with God than how we act at church or at the office.

For example, suppose a couple is struggling over the issues of time and commitment. The husband is deeply committed to his career, often to the point of neglecting his family. The wife is similarly committed to the children.

One Sunday this couple hears a stirring sermon at church. The pastor preaches about the importance of the family and supports his vision with dreadful statistics about divorce and latch-key children.

The couple is touched. They discuss the issue on the way home from church, and the children in the back seat hear their conversation.

As a result of the discussion, the husband commits himself to spend more time with the family. The wife, in turn, commits herself to be more responsive and to stop nagging him.

But within three weeks, they are back in the same old rut. He's late when he has promised to be home in time for dinner with the family. She's angry. The children go to sleep that night before Dad comes home, knowing that something is wrong. You could cut the tension with a knife. And you can imagine the fight that ensues when the husband finally arrives.

If we were to ask the husband and wife what they were fighting about, they would probably agree that it concerns issues of time and family commitment. They both believe family is important. And they both know what they ought to do.

But our assertion is that they aren't focusing upon the real issue: the values that are reflected in their behavior.

The husband is the easy one to pick on. He's committed to his career and gains a great deal of satisfaction from making a name for himself at work. He's on his way up, and his fantasies are finally beginning to be fulfilled. There's no telling how far he can go. The money is just now beginning to make the sacrifices worth it.

This man truly believes he should place priority on his role as husband and father. But he truly values the strokes he receives at work. And when push comes to shove, his career—what he values—wins.

The issue for the wife is less clear. She doesn't realize it, but her commitment to being at home for the children, coupled with her desire to live in the home they can barely afford and in a neighborhood where the schools are exceptional, reflects what's really important to her—and it's not what she believes it is!

It takes a lot of money to live where they do, and according to their arrangement he's responsible for generating the income. When push comes to shove, she would rather have the freedom to be at home with the children in the house and neighborhood she likes than have her husband home on time for dinner.

No matter how they try, they can't have it both ways. They are trapped in the dilemma of the double-minded.

And it happens to all of us at times. We all have treated hatefully those whom we say we love. "Double-mindedness" is a common characteristic of most real-life marriages. What can be done about it?

Our answer to this dilemma is to look hard at what it is we *say* we believe. We become double-minded because somehow our faith and our works become disconnected. In our opinion, the key to reconnecting the two is to focus on values.

The Components of a Values System

In order to understand the concept of values, we would like to begin with a set of definitions, which we'll then put together to form a paradigm or blueprint of how they work together.

The first word we want to define is *object*. An object is

anything to which meaning may be attached. Objects can be material—such as the chair you're sitting in, the book you're reading, or the car you'll drive tomorrow. They can be abstract, as well—such as honesty, truth, justice. Our language system has given us the ability to attach meaning to literally thousands of objects in our world. The objects in the experiences of the couple in the example would include status, recognition, safety, a nice house, comfort—those things in their world to which they attach significance.

Value is the second word we want to define. When we speak of value, we mean the relative degree of significance or insignificance people attach to the objects, whether material or abstract, that make up their world.

We can think of the objects in our lives as being distributed along a kind of continuum of values, which might look something like figure 1.

As the figure shows, the values we attach to the objects in our lives range from very positive to very negative.

Our fictional couple attached to the objects of status, recognition, safety, and comfort a high level of significance—even higher than the significance they attached to their family togetherness—although they "believed" their family was more important. In terms of the realities of their life and marriage, they were double-minded. The bottom line—their behavior—mirrored their actual values, in spite of their verbal statements to the contrary.

Conflict can easily occur in a real-life marriage when one partner attaches positive value to an object which the other views as unimportant or repugnant. For example, early in our

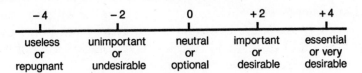

Figure 1
The Continuum of Values

marriage Lucy let it be known that there were certain special occasions which called for celebration—preferably with a gift, or at least a card. Dennis heard what she was saying, but it didn't really register because when he was growing up his family hadn't made much of special occasions. He managed to remember the obvious events such as birthdays and anniversaries, but after the children were born he began to miss some of the others. For several years, Lucy would anticipate the approach of a special occasion such as Valentine's Day with a kind of dread. Would Dennis remember or not? More often than not, in those early years, he didn't.

In terms of our definition, Lucy was attaching a very positive degree of importance to an object—the celebration of special occasions by giving and receiving cards and gifts. On the other hand, Dennis was attaching to that object a neutral importance at best—and more normally, an unimportant significance. The subsequent collision was over more than just how to celebrate family traditions. It was a collision of values systems.

Not until years later, when Lucy was able to explain why the celebration of special occasions was so important to her (it had to do with early childhood experiences) was Dennis able to appreciate the special importance attached to Lucy's view of celebration. Recognizing and accepting what she valued gave Dennis the motivation to work at celebrating life more. For the most part, he has changed and Lucy's appreciation reflects the difference.

The significance of giving and receiving gifts and cards is minuscule when compared to the other values issues over which people come into conflict. Yet, Dennis has had father-and-son clients who got into fist fights over the length of hair. He has seen daughters who have run away from home over conflicts about drugs, and couples have come to the point of divorce over the relative importance of sex.

Understanding how we differ in terms of the value we attach to critical objects in our world is therefore of vital importance.

The third definition we need to make for our blueprint is that of *belief.* Here *belief* is defined as those assertions we make about the objects in our world—statements which can neither be proven nor disproven. Most of us think of the term *belief* in its religious context. For the Christian, our Christian beliefs are deeply important. However, there are many other beliefs, other than the ones that make up our faith, that affect our lives. And both our secular and our religious beliefs have an effect on how we act.

For example, Dennis's grandfather used to say, "The only car worth owning is a Pontiac. The worst of the lot are Fords." No matter what you might say to him, you couldn't budge his belief about cars. He drove a Pontiac until the day he died. He wouldn't even think of buying another kind of automobile. To him, loyalty to Pontiac took the form of a firm belief.

The next definition in our blueprint is that of *attitude.* We would define an attitude as a predisposition to certain behavior—that is, what we think before we act. An attitude is the combination of the values and beliefs which incline us to do certain things.

What is of importance for our discussion is that, even though it is in vogue to talk about "changing attitudes," experts in the social and behavioral sciences agree that "attitudes" are both hard to understand and hard to change. Just the fact that we talk and preach as if we know what we're saying about attitudes doesn't mean we do. The bottom line is that even though your teenager's "attitude" drives you up the wall, pinpointing what that attitude *is* can be pretty complicated—and getting him or her to change that attitude is next to impossible.

Instead of focusing on attitude, then, we would like to concentrate upon a concept that we all can get a handle on: *behavior.* Behavior means, very simply, the acts that we do. We know we are talking about behavior if two people can observe a person and then agree about what they see him or her doing. The reason behavior is important is that we can do something about it. We can change what we do even though our attitude might still be less than what we wish. We can "love our enemy," through our actions, even though our thoughts about him are wrapped up in angry and bitter feelings.

How Values Operate

Figure 2 illustrates how all these definitions fit together in terms of human thought and behavior. The significance of the lines in the diagram is to indicate the relative degree of effect each of the parts of the blueprint have on one another. The dotted line reflects weak effect, the single line reflects moderate effect, and the double line reflects a strong effect.

It is important to realize that, according to this blueprint, the values process is a constantly *interacting* phenomenon, not a linear process of cause and effect. Values have a strong effect

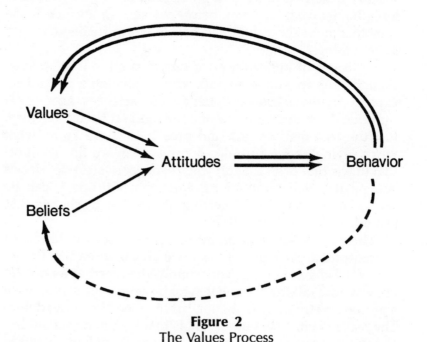

Figure 2
The Values Process

upon our attitudes, which in turn have a strong effect upon our behavior, which in turn strongly reinforces our value system. Beliefs, however, whether they are secular or religious in nature, are weakly affected by our behavior and have only a moderate effect upon our attitudes.

An example might be helpful here. Suppose a recent high school graduate in our church goes off to a secular college. He has been taught both by his church and by his family that the use of recreational drugs such as marijuana is wrong and that it inevitably leads to the use of harder drugs such as heroin. The latter assertion is a *belief*, strongly held by his parents, but not necessarily backed up by the facts. The parents also attach a repugnant value to the use of drugs, although the son is basically neutral on the issue.

When the boy arrives at college during the first semester, he finds that many of his friends in the dorms use marijuana. The new friendship system of which he is now a part attaches optional importance to the use of the drug. When it's passed around at parties, initially he refuses and makes an excuse. But eventually his behavior changes; he tries some. According to our blueprint he can't change his behavior without its having a strong effect upon his values and vice versa.

When the young man returns home at Christmas break, he and his father get into a discussion about college life. Soon the conversation turns to the subject of drugs and quickly turns into a heated argument. The father makes statements about smoking marijuana which reflect his system of values and are supported by his beliefs about the subject. The son counters with statements reflecting his own. The evening ends with the son stalking from the dinner table and disappearing into his room. The parents go to sleep that night deeply afraid. Their son has changed, but they don't know how much. No matter how much they have lectured their son about his attitudes toward drugs and their beliefs about the subject, his behavior and the subsequent reinforcement of a new values system have altered much of what had gone before.

Ought To or Want To?

Perhaps the most important fact shown in the values blueprint is that our values (what we really want) influence our behavior more than our beliefs (what we think we ought to do) influence our behavior. This explains why people can sincerely believe something, yet act in ways that contradict those beliefs. A person can believe in good nutrition while shoveling in candy and potato chips. Or a person can believe in supporting the church and yet fail to make regular contributions. At a practical level, it's our values, not our beliefs, that make the difference in our lives.

We would even go so far as to say that Jesus was crucified by his enemies not because he disagreed with what they believed, but because he disagreed with what they valued. The great conflicts between Jesus and the Pharisees had to do with their attaching essential value to the observance of religious rules, to the neglect and even to the hurt of persons.

For example, Mark records that the Pharisees were concerned more about the precise observance of the Sabbath than they were about the welfare of the man with the withered hand. When Jesus healed the man in the synagogue on the Sabbath, he confronted their values system. And Mark says that they went out after that and began to plot his death. Why? His religious belief system was virtually the same as theirs. He taught traditional Jewish beliefs and believed in the resurrection of the dead in the same way they did. But his values system was radically different from theirs; what was important to him wasn't important to them. Because of that difference, they saw to it that he was killed.

It was for the same reason that Jesus' followers were persecuted just as he had said they would be. In the first century, and the centuries since, Christians have suffered discrimination and even death because their value system differed from the values of those around them.

The same is true today. In some places it's considered appropriate to espouse a religious belief system as long as it doesn't change how you live and what is important to you. But the minute you change how you live and that behavior reflects what is important to you, you can expect resistance and even persecution from others, whether that persecution is subtle or obvious.

For instance, suppose the manager of an industrial plant is religious and reflects his belief system by his attendance at church. Suppose also that there is a problem at his company regarding some mildly toxic industrial waste which would be extremely costly to dispose of legally.

So someone in authority over the plant manager suggests flushing the waste down the sewers in the street, being cautious to do so at night so as not to draw attention to the practice. After all, what's a little contaminant compared with all the pollution that's spewed into the air and water every day?

It's very possible that our industrial manager could "go along in order to get along"; after all, the bottom-line profitability of his company is a basic concern of his. If, however, his belief system and his value system are congruent, he will refuse to go along and in doing so risk losing his job. The dilemma this man faces is whether or not to be double-minded. And he is facing the reality that choosing *not* to be double-minded could mean the kind of persecution Jesus spoke of in the Gospels.

The radical implication of what we are saying is that when it comes to choosing what to do, *our values outweigh our beliefs.*

Implications for Marriage

The logic of what we are saying as it applies to marriage is that "easy believism" in our faith in God leads to "easy believism" in our marriages. What do we mean?

We all make statements about what we *believe* is important when it comes to our marriages. We believe we ought to spend more quality time with one another. We believe we ought to control our temper more, be more sexually responsive, be more financially responsible, and so on. We make promises to ourselves, to one another, and to God to that effect. But, more often than not, we don't change. Why?

Our answer is that in marriage, as in all of life, *if what we want is in conflict with what we believe, then what we want will win.* All of the promises in the world will not change a thing unless we accept responsibility for our behavior in terms of what we want.

Consequently, it's harder to be married to someone who doesn't want what you want than it is to be married to someone who doesn't believe what you do.

This is a somewhat different interpretation of the apostle Paul's teaching about being "unequally yoked" in marriage (2 Cor. 6:14). The emphasis in the church has been almost totally upon the congruence of beliefs and only marginally upon the congruence of values. We are arguing for a greater balance between the two.

Part of the problem, in our opinion, is the tendency to focus on attitudes and beliefs rather than values and behavior. The more basic issue lies with matters of values systems as reflecting what people want rather than with the belief question of what husbands and wives should or shouldn't do.

It is our firm conviction that *greater good will come to a marriage if a couple works at wanting the same things than if they focus only on believing the same things.* This is not to say that beliefs are not important. It is only to say that the kinds of conflicts that divide a marriage are more often conflicts in values than they are conflicts in belief.

Every time a sermon is preached, a film is produced, or a tape is recorded, the challenge presented to a couple about how they should live with one another must address the values component of their relationship. If it doesn't, we end up focusing the couple's attention upon what they can agree on— their beliefs about marriage—but not on what they really must change or accept—their values as they are reflected in their behavior.

In the next chapter, then, we will look at a biblical model for sound values that applies both to our individual lives and to our relationships. And then we will suggest a process to help a married couple learn to communicate about their values.

CHAPTER EIGHT

Wise or Otherwise

Most of us can identify with the struggles elaborated on in the previous chapter between values and belief, belief and behavior. If we take as a given, then, that values are important, that our behavior or actions represent our value systems written in large letters, and that conflict in marriage is more likely to be a conflict of values than a conflict of beliefs, what shall we do about values?

Our suggestion is that we begin by turning to Scripture. As we mentioned in chapter 7, the Book of James has some helpful things to say on the subject of values.

He suggests in chapter 1 of his epistle that it is possible to come to a place in our lives where we suffer from the problem of "double-mindedness." Our interpretation of that dilemma is a person whose beliefs and values have become seriously incongruous. His argument in chapter 2 of his letter is that if we have biblical faith, our works (behavior, in our blueprint) and our beliefs will be in sync.

Then, in chapter 3 of his letter, James gives us a description of the set of values that is congruous with biblical faith and works—the kind of values we can take as normative for a healthy life and healthy relationships. Actually, in this chapter James is describing *two* sets of attitudes and behavior built on two opposite sets of values—one negative and one positive:

> Who is wise and understanding among you? By his good life let him show his works in the meekness of wisdom. But if you have bitter jealousy and selfish ambition in your hearts, do not boast and be false to the truth. This wisdom is not such as comes down from above, but is earthly, unspiritual, devilish. For where jealousy and selfish ambition exist, there will be disorder and every vile practice. But the wisdom from above is first pure, then peaceable, gentle, open to reason, full of mercy and good fruits, without uncertainty or insincerity. And the harvest of righteousness is sown in peace by those who make peace (3:13–18).

James contrasts a lifestyle based on what he calls the "wisdom that is from below," that is, from the earth (vv. 14–16) with a lifestyle based on the "wisdom that is from above," that is, from heaven (vv. 17–18). We have found James's description of the two sets of values very helpful in pinpointing the kinds of values, attitudes, and behavior that make for healthy lives and relationships.

Wisdom from Below

As we saw in chapter 7, values, attitudes, and behavior are all tied closely together. Accordingly, James's description of the "wisdom from below" can be sorted into these three interrelated dimensions—the system of values itself, a set of attitudes that emanate from that system, and a resulting two-fold set of behaviors.

Earthbound Values

According to James, the "wisdom from below" is a values system that is "earthly," "unspiritual," and "devilish" (v. 15).

Earthly has to do with the standards of the world. When viewed by themselves, these standards may appear to be all right to most of us.

We are reminded of a long-running television series that depicted the inner workings of an urban police precinct. Each episode began with a veteran sergeant briefing the officers about the particulars of their shift. They were to be aware of fellow officers on stakeout, other officers operating undercover, and so on.

At the end of his briefing, the sergeant always ended with the same injunction: "Remember, let's do it to them before they do it to us." With that in mind, the squad room would empty and the program would begin.

The injunction "Let's do it to them before they do it to us" has a kind of earthly wisdom. It represents a "survival of the fittest" mentality. But it's not at all Christian.

Unfortunately, the same kind of "wisdom" can influence a marriage, causing a cycle of blaming and defensiveness. It's often difficult to figure out how a fight gets started; it depends on how you punctuate the dialogue. But the result is an endless chain of conflict that leads nowhere. The basic attitude seems to be that life is a struggle, and that you really can't trust the other person to want what's best for you; you've got to take care of yourself by imposing your will on the other. At this level, marriage is experienced as a kind of inner city ghetto, with the object being to survive at all costs.

The second characteristic of a values system that is "from below" is reflected in the word *unspiritual.* The word is translated in other versions as "natural." William Barclay in his commentary on the Book of James, says, "It is the kind of wisdom that makes an animal snap and snarl with no other thought than that of prey or personal survival."*

Note Barclay's phrase, "snap and snarl." We are reminded of the many times in our own relationship when our arguments have sounded like two dogs fighting to the death: the screaming and the yelling, the bitterness and the strife. According to James, at those times we are reflecting a values system that is "natural" and earthbound.

The third characteristic of a values system that is "of the earth" is one that is *devilish,* or demonic. Now, the tendency here is to think of *Exorcist*-like scenes with overtones of witchcraft.

However, in marked contrast, the Scriptures say Satan disguises himself as an "angel of light" (1 Cor. 11:14). His temptation of Jesus in the wilderness (Matt. 4:1–11) is an example of how deceptively attractive he can be. The scene was one of reasonable dialogue; Satan was seductive rather than coercive. His suggestions made sense, given his goals. He tempted Jesus with the offer of sustenance and comfort, power and control, fame and wealth—words that seldom are thought of as being "demonic."

In terms of real-life marriage, think about how much of our lives is spent pursuing the "objects" that Satan offered to Jesus. Sustenance and comfort, power and control, and fame and wealth are not wrong in and of themselves. But they become "demonic" when they become ends in themselves rather than the means to an end.

The chief purpose of the people of God is to glorify him— nothing less. But Satan would seduce us into a lifestyle that makes the accumulation of wealth, the pursuit of comfort, or the seeking after power or recognition our chief ends, rather than the means whereby we glorify God. And that, according to Scripture, is demonic.

*William Barclay, "The Letter from James," *Daily Study Bible* (Philadelphia: Westminster Press, 1960), 109.

Earthbound Attitudes

Using our blueprint, we next focus upon the set of attitudes that James suggests are the result of values "from below." In verse 14, he says that a person who is influenced by the "wisdom from below" must subsequently deal with four attitudes: bitter jealousy, selfish ambition, a boastful spirit, and an orientation toward lying.

The tendency is to think of the most extreme examples of these traits and then deny that they have anything to do with us, because "obviously we're not that bad." But when we look at what James really meant, we can see how easily his words can apply to common attitudes in real-life marriage.

"Bitter jealousy" is a translation of a Greek word from which we derive our English word *zeal*. The connotation is of one who is utterly convinced of his or her own beliefs; the word reflects the zeal with which a person always thinks he or she is right and cannot admit to ever being wrong. Who would ever think that our stubborn insistence that we're right could be a symptom of "bitter jealousy"?

The second attitude of the "wisdom from below" is "selfish ambition." This conjures up a mental image of a person who thinks only of his or her own immediate gain. Such people customarily look after themselves first. Underneath all their actions is the question, "What's in it for me?"

Suppose, for example, that the spouse who is responsible for paying the bills and managing the money (in most families, it is the wife and mother) suffers from "selfish ambition." That spouse will make sure that her special interests are catered to. She may outwardly state that her interests are only in caring for her family, while at the same time juggling the accounts so as to make sure that what she wants will be purchased and/or achieved. ("Selfish ambition" is often the secret skimming of the cream for oneself, unbeknownst to the rest of the family.)

The third attitude, a "boastful spirit," characterizes the people who consistently think they are better than others. They tend to assume superiority over those with whom they have relationships. In our opinion, this attitude is at the heart of what is dreadfully wrong when males dominate females, whites dominate nonwhites, the young dominate the old, or the old dominate the young. Paul's injunction in Galatians 3:28 that "there is neither Jew nor Greek, slave nor free, male nor female, for you are all one in Christ" addresses the problem of a "boastful spirit." In a marriage, whenever the position of one spouse is assumed to be better than the other, for whatever reason, the root cause is often a "boastful spirit."

The fourth and last attitude that results from earthly wisdom is an "orientation toward lying." By this, James is referring to people who represent themselves to be something they're not—usually by trying to make others look bad and themselves look good.

We are reminded of a time, years ago, when Dennis was playing a game of golf with his sixteen-year-old brother-in-law. Dave was clearly the better golfer. However, Dennis had learned at an early age to "psyche out" his competitors. In terms of our illustration, he had learned to present himself in such a way as to make himself look good at the other person's expense.

On the first tee, Dennis just "happened" to mention where the out-of-bounds markers were, hoping that Dave would lose his concentration. Lo and behold, Dave hit his ball into the weeds, taking a two-shot penalty in the process. Dennis, concentrating for all his worth, stepped up to the tee and hit his first ball straight down the fairway. The pattern for the match was set.

By the eighteenth hole, they were playing neck and neck, even though Dave's average was fifteen to twenty strokes better than Dennis's. On the eighteenth hole, Dennis again resorted to his old tactics. The green was elevated and the pin was out of sight. He mentioned to Dave that a bramble of bushes surrounded the far side of the green. At that point Dave hit his ball short of the green and into a trap (a hazard Dennis just managed not to mention). Dennis hit his usual lousy shot and they finished the hole and the game dead even.

As they walked to the car Dave was morose; he had played worse than he had in years. Dennis was satisfied; even though they had tied, he had "won." The ride home was silent. As they approached the house, Dennis mentioned to Dave that Lucy had dinner waiting and would look forward to a time with her "baby brother." But Dave responded with "No, thanks"; he had to get back to his own place. He left on his motorcycle without even a wave.

Later that evening Lucy wondered aloud what had been wrong with her brother. Dennis attributed Dave's behavior to the moodiness of adolescence, but in his heart he knew better.

In the quietness of the evening and in the dark of the bedroom before sleep, Dennis knew he was wrong. It was as if the Holy Spirit rapped him on his knuckles. He had won his golf match with his brother-in-law, but had paid the price in terms of the quality of their relationship. He was a "liar," even though he hadn't told an untruth. And in winning he had lost.

It was more than a year later before Dave would consent to another visit and another game of golf. This time he was ready. On the first tee he smacked the ball three hundred yards straight down the fairway. To Dave's amazement, Dennis cheered and congratulated him for his success. Dennis, in turn, hit his typical errant ball. There was no more psyching his opponent out.

By the time they reached the eighteenth green, Dave was playing one of his better games and Dennis was limping along at his usual pace. Dave birdied the last hole, and Dennis hit his shot into the same sand trap that had snared Dave the last time out. The game was over, and Dave had won. He had played equal to if not better than his average. Dennis had at least finished.

The walk back to the car and the ride back to the house were in marked contrast with the previous trip. Dave chattered the whole way, stayed for dinner, ate his usual seventeen-year-old's second and third helpings of food, and roared off into the night on his motorcycle, buoyed by the success of the day.

REAL LIFE MARRIAGE

In bed that night, Dennis shared with Lucy what had happened that day. Sleep came much easier than it had that other night eighteen months before, because this day had ended not with a lie but with the truth.

It's not hard to find in most of us these attitudes from below. "Always right, never wrong," "What's in it for me?" "I'm better than you," and "Win at any cost" are diseases that gnaw away at the marrow of a relationship, leaving it brittle and susceptible to injury. They are the mark of a heart that is shaped by the "wisdom from below." And seeing them in ourselves is a little like looking in those unflattering three-way mirrors in department store dressing rooms; we are surrounded by images of ourselves that we'd rather not see.

Earthbound Behaviors

The *behaviors* of the "wisdom that is from below" are just as disconcerting as the attitudes when we recognize them in ourselves. James says that those whose values are of the earth live lives marked by "disorder" and "every vile practice."

The disorder he speaks of is in contrast to the natural and normal order which characterize God's creation. God's creation is orderly; sin changes it to chaos and disorder. This is hard to hear. Those of us who are habitually and perpetually disorganized would rather think that these qualities are more winsome than they are worldly. It's hard to admit that the root of our disorganization may lie in a value system that is more characteristic of the world than it is of God.

"Vile practices" refers to those activities which are worthless. James is not necessarily referring to obvious evil here. We would prefer "vile practices" to mean behaviors such as engaging in the commerce of child pornography; that way we can more likely release ourselves from the demands of the passage. But instead, James is referring to the "good-for-nothingness" that can characterize any human behavior. The same words that are used by James here are used in ancient Greek literature to describe a "worthless" flute player who can't get the notes right or a "bad" painter. The emphasis is upon the impossibility of any true gain ever coming from the behavior.

"Vile practices"—it's a description of those of us who feel like we're just "spinning our wheels." It is the meaninglessness of a life filled with activity but with little progress.

Behaviors which are earthbound come in many shapes and sizes. But according to James, what characterizes them all is a tendency toward disorder or chaos and a worthlessness— a lack of purpose and value.

How much of our lives gets filled with just such activity? After a time, we begin to wonder if anything we are doing has any real meaning or significance at all.

One place to begin is to realize that it is possible to live life from day to day and never consider the value system that undergirds it all. Good people with good intentions can find themselves in that kind of a bind. James's injunction is for us to consider the root of the problem: the value system we are living out day to day.

Wisdom from Above

James's description of a values system based on "wisdom from below" is both clear and painfully familiar to most of us; we wince as we recognize ourselves. But of course, James doesn't stop with showing us what negative values are. He goes on to show us a value system based on "wisdom that is from above." These values lead to attitudes and behavior that not only please God, but lead to healthy relationships.

The values system described by James (3:17) is centered around seven characteristics or "objects" (see definition in chapter 7) that are deemed by James to be essential.

Seven Objects of a Heavenly Values System

As we discuss each of these seven objects, ask your-self how important they are to you. In your day-to-day relationships, where do they fit? It may well be that such an evaluation will lead you to realize that you're not as "bad" as you thought you were. Or it might cause you to focus on areas for improvement; you may be called to reprioritize your life in order to place the emphasis on those qualities God thinks are important.

The first object in James's values system "from above" is *"purity."*

The word for purity used by James means freedom from the taint of evil—or morally blameless. It is the most absolute of all the words that connote purity. As such, it refers to a state that is clearly beyond anything we can possibly achieve. We are faced with an object whose value is impossible for us to match or deliver.

This is why we need a relationship with Jesus Christ. He is the righteous or "pure" one. The paradox is that on our own we cannot deliver the only thing God can accept: righteousness. Our value system begins with the knowledge that Jesus Christ is not only the ultimate measurement, but also the ultimate source, of our priorities.

The apostle John said it this way: "Beloved, we are God's children now; it does not yet appear what we shall be, but we know that when he appears we shall be like him, for we shall see him as he is" (1 John 3:2).

The impossible demand of purity, that is, freedom from the taint of evil, has been unalterably met in the life, death, burial, and resurrection of God's son, Jesus Christ. A values system that is from above, therefore, doesn't *end* in heaven; it begins there.

And so the first question we must ask ourselves is, "Do I have a relationship with Jesus Christ?" Only the purity he provides is sufficient. Being one of God's children begins with a personal relationship with his Son—but it doesn't stop there.

John writes that "everyone who thus hopes in him, purifies himself as he is pure" (1 John 3:3). The strong implication is that those who are God's children will value what he values.

In real life, let alone in real-life marriage, purity is usually a forgotten product. Godliness and holiness are not popular themes these days. Why? Perhaps it is because we have separated the part from the whole; to be double-minded is the norm. After all, who wants to be thought of as being "holier than thou"?

Too often we look at ourselves, as well as at others, and realize that we are not doing what we ought to be doing. All of the thundering "oughts" have not changed our "wants." In fact, the emphasis on "oughts," though well-meaning, has left us with a spiritual confusion that permeates the significant relationships of our lives—certainly our relationship with God, and also our relationships with one another in the family.

It is not by accident, then, that James begins his list of the objects of a heavenly values system with purity.

The second object on James's list is *"peaceableness."* Though it is a word that is often used these days, it's a word that needs underlining in the manuscripts of our lives. Whereas James suggests that there is a cruel wisdom which takes delight in hurting others, the wisdom that is from above is the wisdom which brings people closer to one another and closer to God.

We humans often find ourselves in a position where we can function as catalysts in the relationships between others. A catalyst is something that modifies or changes a reaction between two other things without itself being consumed in the process. The question for us as catalysts becomes, when we walk into a room filled with tension and strife, do we make the situation better or do we make it worse? If we sense that our spouse is feeling irritable, do we exacerbate his or her irritability, or do we find a way to lessen it?

Sometimes, just putting our nose where it doesn't belong foments the problem. For instance, if Dad arrives home at the precise moment when Mom is having an argument with one of the kids, does it get better or does it get worse when he arrives? More often than not, being peaceable involves letting the combatants work it out for themselves.

The bottom line is that one who is peaceable is committed to healing rather than to injuring. Knowing when to be willing to yield may well be the best way to chart a peaceable course. At other times peaceableness may mean being willing to take a firm but not intractable stand. *Peace* is an active word, but, it is not intrusive. Knowing the difference often changes the outcome of a tense situation.

The third object on James's list is the word *gentle*. In our culture, the word has come to mean a kind of softness. But in the days of the New Testament, this was not the case. Instead, the word had a connotation of that which is fair and patient.

The ancient Greeks are said to have believed that to be gentle was to be one who steps in to correct things when the law itself becomes unjust. It is the person who knows how to forgive, when strict justice would allow condemnation. It is the person who tempers justice with mercy.

This quality relates to the common problem of the "family pharisee." In a family, the pharisee is the person who would have judgment fall on anyone in the family who has broken the rules—even himself or herself—without ever considering extenuating circumstances.

Children between the ages of eight and ten are notorious for being pharisees. How many times can we remember incidents when children would bellow self-righteously with rage because one of their siblings had broken a rule and the parent seemed to be softening the punishment rather than imposing the full limit of the law! "You always let him get away with it!" "It's just not fair!"

Sometimes, however, a decision needs to be made that recognizes that people are always more important than things. The rules in our families most often center upon what we do or how we treat things. Not tracking mud in from the outside may be important. But feeling comfortable in your own home is important, too. Sometimes the predominance of rules precludes comfort. It's easy to have more rules about things than rules about relationships. To be "gentle" is to recognize that, in the long run, the relationships between the members of the family or marriage are more important than the rules of the home. Gentleness implies placing a higher priority upon people than upon things.

The fourth word on James's list is *reasonableness*. It means being willing to listen, willing to be persuaded, skilled in knowing when to wisely yield.

Parents are reasonable when they make it a practice to encourage their children, particularly their adolescents, to lobby their case with as much evidence and passion as they can muster whenever they are faced with a decision or rule they don't agree with. Reasonableness means letting them sit at the foot of the parents' bed and argue their case about a parental decision that affects them. If they're right, the reasonable parent lets their arguments prevail. The reasonable parent will admit to being wrong, but also sticks to his or her guns when right. The issues of justice and reason are at the heart of most authority issues in families.

Most kids, especially teenagers, want their parents to be reasonable more than they want their own way. They will never learn to be reasonable if parents are not willing to negotiate.

Being reasonable, as James portrays it, also has something to do with being able to admit we're wrong and being willing to make it right.

Both parts of that definition are necessary. For it's easy to get into the habit of quickly admitting we're wrong, but never making it right. This clearly voids the meaning of the supposed repentance, because if our words mean anything, they will lead to a change in our behavior. Repentance without a subsequent change in behavior is only sorrow, and sorrow can be as shallow as the momentary feeling it implies—here today and gone tomorrow.

On the other hand, it's easy to get into the habit of avoiding the admission of one's error, quickly hastening to make right whatever we've done without stopping to apologize. Our partner only learns of our repentant spirit by inference;

they know we know we're wrong because we're acting repentantly. We've changed our behavior but have done so without saying "I'm wrong" or "I'm sorry."

Reasonableness implies both words and actions. To avoid the words because we're embarrassed or because we're proud usually limits the impact of our decision.

Neither extreme is what James means when he encourages us to be "reasonable." The word is like a two-sided coin: one side is to admit you're wrong, the other side is to make it right. If we habitually trade with one-sided coins in relationships, the notion of being reasonable is weakened—if not totally stripped of its meaning.

The fifth object in James's list is a combination of words— we are to be *full of mercy and good fruits*. This has to do with a kind of mercy that results even when the other person has brought the problem upon himself or herself.

We have a friend who, one Christmas, bought her eight-year-old son a new skateboard. Included with it were knee and elbow pads and a helmet. As he rushed out the door she called after him, reminding him to wear the protective gear. His answer was "Sure, Mom."

He proceeded up the street behind their house to a hill that was especially tempting to kids on skateboards. He also promptly shed his pads and helmet.

Wildly he careened down the winding street. And within seconds, he had missed a turn and had "wiped out" into the back of a parked car.

It was a disaster. Skateboard in hand, with blood streaming from a cut forehead and knees and elbows scraped, he came limping home. His mother heard him sobbing as he rounded the walk, and she knew what had happened.

Full of anger, she opened the door, took her son by the hand, and led him down the hall. Turning the corner into the bathroom, she boosted him onto the bathroom counter and opened the medicine chest. Before her stood two bottles: iodine and Merthiolate. Our friend's temptation was to take the iodine, the medicine that would sting the most, and to pour it generously over his wounds. After all, hadn't her son disobeyed the very rules she had insisted on in order for him to be allowed to ride the skateboard?

At that moment, however, she made a decision based upon what James calls "mercy and good fruits." She decided he had suffered enough. And she took the lesser of the disinfectants and soothed his wounds with it.

The kind of mercy James is speaking of here is the kind that issues in practical help—such as in the actions of the good Samaritan. It is a kind of generosity that leads a person to act mercifully even if the payoff for the action is nil.

In marriage, at one time or another we all bring upon ourselves consequences for which an appropriate response would be, "I told you so" or "You made your own bed; now, lie in it." Such a spirit is the opposite of what James is talking about. A response that is "full of mercy and good fruits" is one that takes into account the hurt and embarrassment already suffered. It doesn't insist upon personal vindication. Sometimes compassion rather than punishment is the best response.

The sixth object suggested by James is an *unwavering quality*. Of all the characteristics mentioned by James as making up the values system that is from above, this value is the one which is most opposite of the characteristic of being "double-minded."

In verse 1:6, James writes that we are to be "with no doubting, for he who doubts is like a wave of the sea that is driven and tossed by the wind." This is a picture of turmoil and instability. In contrast, to be unwavering is to be steady, operating according to settled absolutes.

Just as a navigator steers by the North Star, the unwavering person has settled upon those values and beliefs by which he or she intends to chart his or her life. An unwavering person knows the difference between being stuck and being steady. At the other end of the continuum, they know the difference between chaos and change.

The seventh, and last, object James suggests as describing the wisdom that is from above is *a lack of hypocrisy*. This is the quality of being real—not plastic, not phony. It is a quality that is often lacking in our culture.

Dennis and Lucy both work at the same seminary. Lucy is Director for Student Concerns, and Dennis is Director of the Marriage and Family Ministries program. One of the best things about where we work are the hundreds of students from the Third World who study at our seminary.

One day Lucy was walking across the campus and happened upon one of the African students. "How are you?" she asked, offering a routine greeting of our American culture. "I'm not so good," replied the student, who then proceeded to disclose why he was so upset.

After nearly half an hour, the conversation ended with the African student meandering on his way and Lucy walking off marveling at the differences in the two cultures. What had happened was that the student assumed that, as it was in his culture, so it would be in America: don't ask if you don't want to know, and if you ask, be prepared to take the time to listen. The student had assumed that Lucy's question was without hypocrisy.

In a marriage, we often ask our questions not really wanting to hear the answer. "Are you mad?" or "Did I hurt your feelings?" we inquire, when the only reply we want to hear is, "Don't worry. I'm all right." When our spouse has the audacity to disclose anger or hurt, our response is to become defensive or to counterattack.

Whatever James means, such responses are not "without hypocrisy." Perhaps we should learn from our African friend: Don't ask if you don't want to know. And if you do ask, be prepared for what you hear.

Seeds and Soil

If the wisdom from above is as James suggests, what then are the attitudes and behaviors that would reasonably follow?

In James 3:18, he writes, "And the harvest of righteousness is sown in peace by those who make peace."

James is highlighting one fact: peace means right relationships between persons, whether they be husband and wife or parent and child. It implies a state of uninterrupted fellowship. James summarizes the value system given in verse 17 under one heading and calls it "righteousness." And according to our values blueprint, the value system of righteousness, with all of its multiplicity, then interacts with a set of behaviors he calls "sowing in peace by those who make peace." The key is the interaction between the two; remember, values affect behaviors, and behaviors in turn affect values.

Assuming we all want the rewards of a good life, what will bring this about?

James answers with a metaphor from the farm. There is an interactive relationship between the seeds, the soil, and the harvest. Righteousness is the harvest that comes when we are committed to peace. If we create any other kind of atmosphere, we risk destroying the harvest.

William Barclay says that "right relationships are the soil in which the reward of righteousness can grow. And the only people who can sow these seeds, and who will reap the reward, are those whose life work it has been to produce such right relationships."*

It is just this reasoning that led us to assert in the previous chapter that how we relate to one another at home, in our marriages and with our children, is a better mirror of our relationship with God than what we say and do at church.

James places the emphasis where it needs to be placed. Nothing good comes when we are perpetually and habitually at variance with one another. Bitterness, strife, and wrath are the ingredients of the barren soil that produces little of eternal worth and value. People who insist on living according to the "wisdom from below" will reap what they have sown.

In contrast, those who work at living according to the "wisdom that is from above" reap an unusual harvest. Their

*Barclay, "The Letter from James," 114.

commitment to peace or right relationships yields the best of all rewards for the Christian, the reward of righteousness.

A Couple's Values Conference

In writing about the issue of values as they are discussed in James's letter, we became aware that any discussion between a couple about what we have said could easily deteriorate in a chaotic argument. After all, when we talk about values, we're talking about what's really important, and strong feelings can be evoked.

In order to preempt such a problem, we'd like to establish some guidelines for a couple's discussion of these issues.

We first discovered a variation of this process in the late 1960s in a lecture by Dr. Raymond Corsini of the University of Hawaii. We have used the method several times throughout the years and have adapted the process for our own purposes.

One word of caution: the more strongly either partner feels about an issue the more important it is that they *follow our suggestions to the letter.*

1. Read the material found in chapters 3 and 4 separately before you discuss it together.

2. Decide together to have a Values Conference. The rule would be that if either partner wants a conference, that's enough reason to have one.

3. Choose a time and place to meet when the two of you will be reasonably rested and when you can expect to be uninterrupted. (The Values Conference will only take a total of thirty minutes in fifteen-minute sessions.)

4. In a quiet room, set two chairs back to back. The reason for this is the need to circumvent all of the nonverbal communication cues that have been developed between you through the years. Expect some initial

discomfort in the process. This will diminish as you progress.

5. Set a timer for five minutes. Flip a coin to decide who goes first. The first person talks for five minutes about his or her values or the values of the marriage or family (or about any other issue he or she deems to be important). The other person only listens. There is to be no interaction—only speaking and listening. Try as much as you can to stay on the subject. But no matter what, do not interrupt.

6. When the bell rings, the second person's turn begins, and he or she talks for five minutes. The other person only listens. Focus on making statements, and avoid asking questions.

7. When the timer rings after the second five minutes, reset it for five minutes and let the first speaker talk again. This person can choose to respond to whatever he or she has heard. Or this person can choose to open up new subjects.

8. When the bell rings, signaling the end of the fifteen-minute conference, leave the room and go your separate ways. Don't interact for at least one hour; this will allow for any anger to subside and hurt feelings to ebb. When you do come back together again, it's best to talk of other things.

9. Make an appointment for the second half of the conference, which should be at least twenty-four hours later. Repeat the same format exactly, but this time reverse the order of speakers, with the second person going first this time. Don't deviate from this process, even if you think you know better.

10. Repeat the process as long as it seems to be working. And don't give up too soon; give it a chance. The ideal would be a three- to four-week commitment to hold at least two fifteen-minute conferences per

week. Our experience is that couples who are having difficulties usually find it hard to take even thirty minutes a week to sit down and talk about the things that are important to them. If that happens, try not to make this an issue with one another. Schedule what you can, and try to hold up your end of the commitment.

11. If either of you finds that the process has become destructive, not just hard, find a counselor you can trust and go together for professional help. It's better to be safe than sorry.

Our experience with the Couples Values Conference has been that after awhile it becomes integrated into the way a couple communicates about hard issues—values then take their appropriate place as the major component in behavior and decision making. Whenever in the future you find yourself facing a hurdle you can't get over as a couple, the Values Conference format can work as a tool to help you reestablish communication and start pulling together again.

As with every issue of real-life marriage, synchronizing your values and keeping communication about values open takes real work. The results are worthwhile in terms of heightened closeness and reduced conflict, but the process will take commitment and dedication. But this is true of any human relationship; we believe it is what God expects of human beings. And so we close with this marvelous quote from the prophet Zechariah:

> These are the things that you shall do: Speak the truth to one another, render in your gates judgments that are true and make for peace, do not devise evil in your hearts against one another, and love no false oath, for all these things I hate, says the Lord (Zech. 8:16–17).

We wish you well as you meet together in the gate.

CHAPTER NINE

The Life-Cycle
Squeeze

When Dennis wrote *Thoroughly Married* ten or so years ago, the book's topic of sexual communication in marriage was appropriate to where we were as a couple. We had been married fifteen years, and we were in our late and middle thirties.

We've now been married for more than twenty-five years. Dennis is in his late forties and Lucy is in her middle forties. And we find that the topic of this book is especially appropriate to the issues with which we are dealing now. This chapter in particular is relevant for us. It has to do with life cycles—the predictable and normal changes a couple goes through as they live out their lives day to day, month to month, and year to year.

The concept of a family life cycle has been around for about twenty years. It was generated in order to describe how and why families develop throughout their history together. Family sociologists observed that a typical family goes through at least seven stages, each beginning with a predictable crisis brought about by the introduction of a new role demand in the family. How well or how poorly the family was prepared to navigate the crisis determined how they fared in it.

The selection of the word *crisis* is significant here. It indicates that tension is central to the concept of the life cycle. What this tells us is that it is *normal* for families in general and couples in particular to experience times of dis-ease, even dysfunction, in their history together. The road to development as a family is marked by predictable potholes. There is no such thing as a perfectly smooth ride.

You'll note that we've used the word *squeeze* in the title of the chapter. By this we mean to imply that, as a couple moves through the predictable stages of the life cycle, a kind of pressure develops—a pressure that places demands upon them physically, socially, spiritually, and especially financially. Most couples disregard the significance of this pressure and, as a result, pay the price. It's our hope that with a better understanding of the "squeeze" you're in will come some form of relief.

As you read this chapter and identify the stage you're in, we suggest that you ask yourself these questions: Were you prepared to handle the demands of your present stage? How well are you prepared to handle the next stage? And how are your actions or your inaction facilitating or hindering the development of those in your own family—yourself and your spouse as well as your children?

The stages of the family life cycle, in chronological order, are: (1) the young single adult who is "between families," (2) the newly married couple, (3) the couple with their first baby, (4) the couple with their first school-aged child, (5) the couple with their first teenager, (6) the couple whose last child has left home, and (7) the couple in retirement.

Notice that each successive stage in the life cycle of the family demands that the couple function in new roles and use a new set of skills. Understanding the demands of these new roles and learning the necessary skills that are the critical tasks the couple must carry out in order to negotiate the stage successfully.

Stage 1: The Between-Families Young Adult

Central to this stage of development is establishing a sense of personal identity and autonomy. Can we make it on our own, or do we need to be sustained by our parents as a "pseudo-adult," playing at being a "grown up"?

The issue of *identity* involves the ability to conceive of yourself as a person in your own right, separate and distinct from those with whom you grew up. It involves moving out from under the shadow of parents and siblings, having a realistic sense of who you are, being free to take the risks associated with real life so as to experience your own sense of success or failure, and developing your own personal relationship with God.

This particular issue has been hard for Lucy to negotiate. When she first moved away from home, she took up residence in a college dorm and began to develop an identity of her own. The problem, however, was that in those days it wasn't considered appropriate for a young woman to be a person in her own right—at least not in the Christian circles in which Lucy was raised. It wasn't considered "appropriate" for her to have dreams and aspirations of her own. So, she did what many young women did at that time; she tied her aspirations to the dreams of a husband. She tied her future to Dennis's.

It meant that when she got married, she had to work through two agendas simultaneously. She had to find herself as a person, and she had to adapt to the role demands of being a wife and, eventually, a mother. What it meant, in practical terms, was that she deferred until later in life her own development as a person independent of a family. It also meant that in the interim she experienced times of frustration—frustration that often was masked in a general dissatisfaction with herself, with Dennis, and with the marriage. Later on, as she progressively discovered herself as a person, the frustration and dissatisfaction lessened. She was a much happier person to be around. Dennis could tell the difference, as could the others in the family.

The idea of *autonomy* involves supporting yourself both functionally and financially. It has to do with taking care of yourself and not being dependent upon the care of others.

If Lucy's struggle in this stage of the life cycle was one of identity, Dennis's struggle was one of autonomy. In practical day-to-day terms, Dennis had always been "taken care of" by his mother and grandmother. It's embarrassing for him to admit it, even today, but before he married he had rarely washed his own clothes, cooked for himself, or managed the practicalities of life.

Dennis, then, deferred the responsibilities of functional autonomy until much later in the marriage, just as Lucy deferred working out her own identity. To Dennis, financial autonomy was easy enough to come by; functional autonomy was not. (And again this was related to cultural expectations of men's and women's roles.) Like Lucy, Dennis had two issues to work out simultaneously early on in our marriage. He had to learn to take care of himself at the same time that he was learning to take care of his family.

The demands this placed on Lucy compounded the struggles she was having in terms of her own self-identity. If Dennis wasn't able to cook for himself, to wash his own laundry, or to organize the pragmatics of life, Lucy had to do it all. And she had to do it at the expense of her own agenda.

The net result for our marriage was a kind of collusion that "got us off the hook" in terms of the necessary tasks. We tacitly agreed that Dennis would take care of the identity for the relationship and Lucy would take care of the autonomy. Neither of us had to "grow up"; we could depend upon each other. In this sense, for many years of our marriage we were both pseudo-adults, pretending we were "grown up" while all the time depending upon each other to balance the scales of our own development.

Like many other couples who marry young, we have had to grow up together. The twin tasks of developing identity and autonomy were finally learned, but the price was a greater level of frustration than was necessary. It's better to grow up before you marry, not after.

Stage 2: The Newly Married Couple

This stage involves learning the new role of being a spouse.

The major tasks associated with being newly married can be summed up in the concepts of "leaving" and "cleaving." We take "leaving" to involve the issues of developing a sense of one's own identity, and the ability to function autonomously— especially if this was deferred from the previous stage, as it was in our case. We take "cleaving" to mean the ability to un- conditionally commit oneself to another and the capacity to relate intimately to each other.

Since we've already focused two chapters on the issues of intimacy and commitment we'll not labor the point further, except to underline the fact that there is more to getting mar- ried than just being old enough to sign the marriage license. "Leaving and cleaving" involves the development of an iden- tity as a couple—separate and distinct from that of our families of origin.

When we think of this principle, we are reminded of the words of the family psychiatrist, Carl Whitaker. According to Whitaker, a wedding can be defined as "two families sending forth a scapegoat to reproduce themselves."

We think Whitaker's point, while humorously stated, is well taken, and it is important to understanding this stage of the life cycle. A major task facing the newly married couple involves developing a loyalty to one another in the face of the existing loyalties to their families of origin. It involves establishing their own traditions: the first Thanksgiving turkey they've cooked by and for themselves, Christmas presents under their own tree, etcetera.

For the couple's parents this is sometimes hard. It involves "letting go," and letting go can be difficult. For example, it can involve sharing sons or daughters with their in-laws rather than having them at home with you for the holidays. It involves blessing the new marriage by keeping your advice to yourself even when you *know* you know better than the couple. It involves watching them struggle to make it on their own, financially and functionally, helping if, and only if, the help is needed and asked for. It also involves keeping your nose out of their relationship when they have problems getting along, as they inevitably will.

By this time, the gathering forces of the life-cycle squeeze begin to form. In the early phases of the marriage, it involves the confluence of many pressures, pressures which come from other people as well as from the new relationship itself. But the greatest pressure is yet to come.

Stage 3: The Couple with Their First Child

Almost as much romanticism has formed around becoming a parent, especially a mother, as has formed around getting married. Many women in our culture feel they are not a "real woman" until they have had a child. Unfortunately, the romanticized myth of parenthood doesn't tell the whole story, which involves some hard realities as well as fantasies.

The fantasy of parenting is true, in part, in that those early years with a first baby can be very fulfilling. But it's also true that most of us are required to drastically alter our lives with his or her coming. Why? Because with the coming of the first child, new realities must be faced.

For many young parents, the romance of being a new

mother or a new father is lost in the realities of postpartum depression, financial pressures from child-care expense or from learning to live on one income after having become accustomed to a lifestyle supported by two, and the ever-present fact of physical fatigue. Coupled with all of this is the fact that the new baby is an ingenious intruder. All manner of marital habits must change, including, but not limited to, sleeping and sexual patterns. Life will never be the same.

Stage 3 of the family brings a whole new set of pressures and problems along with the wonder and joy. Yet if new parents admit to an ambivalence about parenthood, they risk censure by those who teach that being a mother or a father is the ultimate state of grace.

In our opinion, new parents would be better served if society and the Christian community faced up to the facts.

What are the facts? Writing in the prestigious *Journal of Marriage and the Family,* Dr. Carlfred Broderick, Professor of Family Sociology at the University of Southern California, reports the following: "The major research finding of the late 1960s and early 1970s was that *children are a detriment to marital satisfaction*" (our emphasis). Said in another way, children are hard on marriage, a fact with which we both agree.

But lest we sound too cynical, we'll explain what we mean.

In the first place, most couples are barely trained to become spouses, let alone parents. It strikes us as paradoxical that as Christians we place great emphasis upon getting married, and we frequently support this emphasis by requiring that couples submit to premarital counseling in order to be married in our churches. Well and good. And yet our emphasis upon becoming successful parents is almost totally unsupported in terms of any formal counsel or training. In our opinion, the major reason children are hard on marriage is that most couples are dreadfully unprepared for the realities of parenting.

The second reason follows closely upon the first. It is that the pressure to be "a good parent" easily leads young couples to neglect their marriages in the pursuit of becoming responsible parents. And, let's face it, the newborn infant happily supports the emphasis. Babies are appropriately narcissistic; as far as they are concerned, the world revolves around their needs. They are demanding creatures. But a young couple needs to be reminded that in the same way it takes two to make a baby, it takes two to make a marriage, and it is the marriage that grows the baby. Children are deeply affected by the nature and quality of the marital relationship. But if all the effort goes into taking care of your baby, the relevant question becomes, who is taking care of your marriage?

The third reason children are hard on marriage has to do with the isolation many couples experience when faced with the demands of their new child. The norm now is for young couples to face the realities of coping with their first child without the support of nearby extended families.

In this sense, the underdeveloped countries of the world are far ahead of us. In those cultures, it is common for the extended families, especially the grandmothers, to be actively involved in the first years of a child's life. Young mothers are not expected to cope with the demands of a new infant alone; someone is always there to help. Someone else gets up in the middle of the night and ministers to the crying baby's needs. The work doesn't all fall on the shoulders of the new mother and father.

Inadequate preparation, disproportionate emphasis upon parenting at the expense of the marriage, and isolation from family support are the down side of parenting in the early years. The result experienced by many of us is a level of stress which results in a predictable loss of marital satisfaction.

In our opinion, the church could do more than it's doing when it comes to supporting the young couple at this stage of the family life cycle. Parenting training can be as important to the success of a marriage as is premarital counseling. And practical help in the form of baby-sitting and giving housebound mothers a break would encourage couples to keep their marriages fresh and alive. (The "Parents Day Out" programs run by many churches are a welcome step in this direction.)

Practical help of this kind, coupled with a church's commitment to becoming "family" to one another, would go a long way to ensuring that a couple with their first child never feels alone as they struggle to learn the basics of parenting while keeping their relationship strong.

Stage 4: The Couple with Their First School-Aged Child

The task that a couple must accomplish in this stage is not the learning of a new role but the changing of one. It is the beginning of the task of "deparenting." The young couple must learn to relinquish the effective control of their first child to others—in this case, the school—at least temporarily. Someone else will have the child more of his or her waking hours than the parents will. The issue becomes whether parents can trust others with their child as well as they trust themselves.

The message the child internalizes is whether or not the external world is to be trusted or distrusted. Is it a place of dread to be feared and avoided, or is it a place to be experienced and enjoyed? Years later, when it comes time to leave home and become an autonomous adult, the message internalized during these formative years will replay itself in the young adult's unconscious. Successful deparenting, even at this early stage, is necessary to produce a confident and independent adult.

Another vital aspect of the parenting task at this stage is supporting the child in his or her learning career. These are the formative years in a child's intellectual development, and the importance of the parents' task at this point can be disguised by the simplicity of the tasks involved. Reading with a young child, supplying materials for artwork, helping with memory drills, and maintaining supportive contact with the child's school are not all that hard, although finding time to do them may be. And they are vital to a child's future.

A whole attitude and approach to life is at stake in these important early years, and neglecting the parental task at this stage can be very detrimental to the child's later development. The parents who anxiously hold on to rather than letting go of a child communicate their anxiety to the child, who in turn will tend to approach the world anxiously. And the parent who approaches learning casually or lethargically will impart those attitudes to the child and hinder his or her later intellectual development.

Stage 5: The Couple with Their First Adolescent

This fifth stage is, practically speaking, the hardest for most parents. And again, research measuring marital satisfaction is clear and consistent. Couples commonly report that their satisfaction with each other and with their marriage is at its lowest ebb during this stage. (We'll go into specifics about this in the next chapter.)

The major task during this stage in the life cycle is to continue the process of deparenting. But there is a major difference. In the previous stage, deparenting involved relinquishing control of the child to the school. In this stage, it involves relinquishing control to the teenager himself or herself. This can be a frightening thought. Just at the time when your kid seems to be the biggest "airhead" in town, you need to consciously relinquish the reins of their life to him or her!

But the tasks at this stage involve much more than "advanced" deparenting. For at no other time in our lives are we so challenged at personal, marital, financial, and spiritual levels.

In terms of the *personal* level, everything we failed to

work out with our own parents when we were teenagers tends to bubble to the surface during these years. If we struggled with our parents' authority, we can expect to struggle with our teenager in the same area. If our parents had trouble accepting our sexuality, we can expect to have similar difficulties accepting our teenager's sexuality.

On top of coping with an adolescent, during this stage some men and women face what has become known as a "midlife crisis." This is a time of restlessness and deep personal dissatisfaction. One writer says it happens when the years a person has left on the earth are fewer than the years he or she has been here. A kind of mental alarm goes off—an alarm that seems to demand changes. Midlife is a time when many people change careers or even marital partners. The strong temptation during this time is to make major transitions without carefully counting the cost and weighing the consequences.

The *marital* challenges during this time can be difficult as well. Adolescents are intuitive and skillful manipulators who often pit one parent against the other, and the personal conflicts of midlife add to the already high stress levels. If there are unresolved issues in the marriage, they will probably surface in spades during this stage. Old resentments may reappear as open wounds. Whatever wasn't working before becomes hurtful and destructive now, and poor communication yields its requisite distance. And because the parents are embroiled in their own problems, the adolescents escape the accountability they need in order to develop into responsible young adults.

Financially, most parents are unprepared to handle the strain of raising teenagers. Studies commissioned by the United States Department of Labor chronicle the financial squeeze families find themselves in during this stage. This financial pressure is affected by two factors: the ages of the children and the size of the family.

What it boils down to is this: If you have a family of four

or more children, the oldest of whom is an adolescent still living at home, it takes *three times* the income to support your family than it takes to support a married couple with no children. That's right—three times! The pressures are lessened or increased depending upon the number and ages of the kids, but the fact remains that there is more financial stress for families at this stage than at any other.

Adding to these pressures is the common expectation that we're supposed to be moving up in the world to bigger and better houses and cars. The result is one gigantic financial headache for many families. This helps explain why so many couples almost come to blows over money during these years. (It also explains why couples are deciding to have fewer children and why so many mothers are working outside the home.)

In *spiritual* terms, raising an adolescent demands a new kind of reliance upon God. A dear friend of ours passed on a piece of advice that helped us through the teen years. She said, "There comes a time when you can no longer physically intervene in your child's life. That is when they are teenagers. And it is then that you must be able to intervene spiritually." Having adolescents drives parents to their knees before God more often than at any other time in their lives. It is a question of learning to trust. Will God go with our teens when they go away from us? If we can't trust *them,* can we trust God?

Charles Dickens begins his novel, *A Tale of Two Cities,* by saying, "It was the best of times and it was the worst of times." The same can be said of the teenage years and of the parents' marriage during those years. For many couples, this stage turns out to be the greatest crisis of all. In a sense, it is the worst of times.

But teenagers can bring out the best in life as well. It can be a joy to see adolescents grow up and mature into responsible young adults—and most of them do, much to the amazement of their parents. The personal, marital, financial, and spiritual issues can be weathered and the marriage can emerge from the crisis of the fifth stage in family life better than ever.

Stage 6: The Couple Whose Last Child Has Left Home

This is the time of the "empty nest." And, according to the same studies that report the greatest marital dissatisfaction during the previous stage, there is usually a strong upturn in satisfaction during this stage. The major task during this stage is the task of readjusting to one another as a married couple. It is a time of launching children into lives of their own and developing relationships with them as friends rather than as parents. It is also the time when the fun of grandparenting begins.

But this is not to say there are no pressures at this stage in the family life cycle. This is a time when many couples must face the reality of aging parents. Just when a couple has launched their last kid, they are faced with the demands of caring for ill or infirm parents—and many couples feel as if they have little children to cope with again. And on top of that, parents at this stage are increasingly caught in the middle as grown children—unable to make a living in today's competitive society—move back home.

Stage 6 is also a time for coming to grips with our own mortality, a mortality that is evidenced by physical and emotional changes. During these years, friends who were always vital and active begin to decline in health, and die. Death, an enemy once so distant, now seems to lurk right around the corner.

Physically, at this stage we can't do what we once could. Emotionally, we become aware of our need for closeness and companionship. For many people, it's as if the axis of the earth has shifted and the issues that once controlled our lives are not so important anymore. Stage 6 is a time of reevaluation and reconciliation, a time to put things right if they're wrong and to make things better if they're bad.

Stage 7: Retirement

The role change that is central in this stage is the change in the occupational or career role. As more and more women join the work force, this role change, once the sole domain of men, is now shared by both men and women. And even a couple in which only the husband works will face stresses brought on by retirement.

Living with less and coping with loss are the dominant themes of these years. Whether it is less income or less time left, loss of occupational productivity or loss of a spouse through death, these tasks demand personal flexibility at a time when both old bones and old thinking tend to calcify. Remaining flexible as a thinking and feeling person is the best way to stay young at heart even if you're growing old in body.

The quality that seems most to buoy the heart during the retirement years is the quality of personal hope. Even though faith is consistently important throughout the life cycle, most people find it especially vital at this time.

Earlier we quoted what Lucy's grandmother used to say about becoming more of what you really are the older you get. Grandma also used to say that she was ready to die and go to heaven because she knew that there she could rest and no longer be tired, and that she could be at peace and hurt no more. Only those who "rest in Jesus" can speak such words of comfort and hope. And that is a hope strong enough to sustain us throughout all the stages of a real-life marriage.

CHAPTER TEN

Good Enough Is Good Enough

In the last chapter we noted that research in the area of marriage and the family consistently indicates that children are hard on marriage. We may not like what the researchers say, but we must take it seriously.

In this chapter we'll look at the task of parenting from the perspective of what can be done about easing some of the pressure. And we'll begin at the beginning by examining the cultural and psychological assumptions about parenting that drive us so hard. Then we'll talk about the myth of perfection, which affects the goals we establish for ourselves. Last of all, we'll offer an alternate perspective—the concept of "good enough," and some suggestions for making the concept work in the real world of real families.

Challenging the Freudian Factor

The problem of escalating idealism happens with families in general and parenting in particular, just as it happens in marriage. We romanticize what it means to be an ideal family, an ideal mother, an ideal father. Then, when we fall short of the ideal, we feel defeated. "Good" isn't great, so we feel it must be bad.

How did we come to such a place in our thinking? We think the whole idea can be traced back to Sigmund Freud, who wrote and practiced in the early years of the twentieth century.

To begin with, we need to realize that Christians as a group have been influenced by Sigmund Freud and his followers just as much as any secular group of people in our culture. Freud's influence on psychology and thought was so singular and profound that it has pervaded our cultural thinking; it is almost impossible to live in twentieth-century Western culture and *not* be influenced by him.

It was not until Freud that the total responsibility for a person's emotional development was laid at the feet of the parents.

Freud's influence led to the assumption that *whether a person becomes a healthy, successful person is the total responsibility of the parents.* In this view, if a child acts up, it is the parents' fault. If a teenager is rebellious, then something is wrong with the mother and/or the father. If you believe this or teach this (or assume it), you are essentially a Freudian, whether you want to accept it or not. We believe that this view is faulty.

In support of our position, we would like to discuss three verses from the Old Testament which must be taken into account when we teach about parenting and the responsibility that goes with it.

For example, in the law as recorded in Deuteronomy 24:16, Moses says, "The fathers shall not be put to death for the children, nor shall the children be put to death for the fathers: every man shall be put to death for his own sin."

Again, when it came time for children who were rebellious to be disciplined, Moses counseled the parents to bring the child (probably a rebellious teenager) to the elders of the city. It's important to note that it is *the elders, not the parents,* who were to discipline the child (see Deut. 21:18). It's also important to note that the elders, in performing this discipline, were functioning as the personification of the community. The community, not the parents, was ultimately responsible for the behavior of the children.

Later Ezekiel emphasized personal responsibility when he wrote, in a similar context, "The son shall not suffer for the iniquity of the father, nor the father suffer for the iniquity of the son; *the righteousness of the righteous shall be upon himself, and the wickedness of the wicked shall be upon himself"* (Ezek. 18:20, emphasis added).

We believe it is essential that the burden of responsibility for how children "turn out" not be laid solely upon the shoulders of parents. Doing so is likely to compound their difficulties and exacerbate their problems, and the community may be guilty of avoiding its own responsibility as well.

We recognize that what we have said earlier in this book might be interpreted in just such a way. Our emphasis upon early bonding between parents and children as a significant building block in the development of intimacy could be interpreted as Freudian. This is not our intent.

Instead, we'd like to argue for the balanced position that while parents are essential in the raising of children, their influence isn't absolute and total. Other factors come into play as well—factors such as the media, inadequate preparation for parenting, the isolation of parents in the raising of their young, genetic predisposition, and the pervasive influence of peer pressure on youth are influential too. It's just not easy to be a parent in this day and age.

The second assumption that adds to the pressure parents

experience in the raising of their children is also related to Freud's influence. It has to do with a one-way view of parenting. By this we mean *the belief that parents influence children and not vice versa.* But anyone who has been a parent knows that family influence is a two-way street. Some children are easier to raise than others. Some kids seem to raise themselves. Others occupy most, if not all, of our parental time and energy from the beginning. You can only hope that you and they both survive until they become adults.

What do we mean when we say that parenting is a two-way street?

This idea has somewhat radical implications. That is that children, very early, must be taught to share in the responsibility for the quality of relationship they have with their parents. Just as parents influence children, children can influence parents.

The ratio is weighted heavily toward the parents when the children are very young and shifts gradually as the children grow older. By the time they reach their early teens, the responsibility approaches a balance, and by the time they are in their late teens and ready to be launched into the adult world, the ratio of responsibility is more or less fifty-fifty.

Just as children bear some responsibility for their relationship with God, so it is with their relationship with parents. As they become older, the responsibility for their relationship with him increases, and in God's eyes they are culpable. That is, whether or not they accept or reject his grace is their responsibility.

We are arguing that what is true in a young person's relationship with God is true as well in his or her relationship with their parents. Families are shared communities with the responsibility for success and failure resting upon broader foundations than just the shoulders of the parents. All who live under the shelter of our roofs, including our children, must learn to bear some of the responsibility for what goes on.

The net effect is to remove some of the terrible feelings of responsibility and guilt many parents carry when it comes to the lives and behaviors of their children and teenagers. If something goes wrong, it's not always totally the parents' fault. The parents definitely bear some responsibility, but they do not bear it all.

The two Freudian assumptions—that parents are totally responsible for how their children turn out as adults, and that parenting is a one-way street—lead to a deadly scenario played out in the day-to-day drama of family life. And this scenario centers upon the myth of the perfect parent.

The Myth of the Perfect Parent

There is a strange parallel between those who demand perfection of themselves as Christians and those who demand perfection of themselves as parents. In the first instance, if we expect perfection of ourselves as Christians and then fall short, we have three alternatives: we can become discouraged and defeated, we can pretend we're perfect even though we know we're not, or we can avail ourselves humbly of the grace and forgiveness of God.

The very fact that this option exists underlines the reality that, although we are urged to strive for perfection, we will never achieve it on this earth according to Scripture.

But what happens when people fail to avail themselves of grace and forgiveness and keep on expecting themselves to be perfect? They must fall back on the first two options, and neither is healthy.

We are reminded of two women friends who lived near us when we were in our first year of seminary. Both were Christians. Both expected perfection of themselves in their walk with God.

One of these women—we'll call her Norma—worked very hard to be all that she could be for God, only to come face to face with her failures. Her response was to vacillate between depression and victory. Her imperfections dominated her relationship with God. She seemed to be constantly trying harder and harder, only to fail again and again. The result was a pervasive and continuing depression.

The second, whom we'll call Marie, worked every bit as hard in terms of her relationship with God, except that she had learned to handle her imperfections differently. She pretended they didn't exist. She defined them away. She seemed to think she had reached "sinless perfection."

In fact, we happened to call on Marie one day and found her in the backyard, burning leaves in an open fire and shielding the flames so they couldn't be seen from the street. Dennis mentioned that open fires were illegal and asked if it didn't bother her that she was breaking the law. Her response was consistent with her belief in "sinless perfection." She explained that the law was silly and that her actions were valid. She claimed to obey God rather than man. She completely denied her responsibility to the law and went on living as if she were perfect, even though she wasn't.

Some people approach the task of parenting much as Norma approached the task of living the Christian life. When faced with the realities of their failures as parents, they become defeated and depressed. They retreat into a vale of hopelessness.

Other parents deny their fallibility through a pretense of perfection, just as Marie did. They don't make mistakes. It's always someone else's fault—usually the child's. Or the problem is only a matter of interpretation. They only "want what's best" for their children and shouldn't be challenged or confronted.

Because this point is so important, we'll illustrate exactly what we mean.

Several years ago, Dennis was asked to become involved with a family whose only son, a young adult, had been diagnosed as schizophrenic.

As therapy progressed, it became obvious that several decisions that had been made very early in the young man's life had been crucial. The mother's decision to divorce the boy's father and her subsequent decision to remarry had especially affected him.

When the mother remarried, the stepfather and the son never really hit it off. In addition, every time the stepfather and the son would come into conflict, the mother would side with the stepfather against the son. She was the dependent type and felt she just couldn't risk another divorce and the threat of being alone. Even when the stepfather became physically abusive with her and the boy, she would defend his actions and berate the son for creating problems.

Psychologically, the son could have handled even the abuse if it hadn't been for the double bind she put him in. When the boy would protest the stepfather's actions and the mother's defense of him, the mother would vehemently insist that what she wanted most of all was her son's happiness. Everything she had ever done as a mother was "in his best interest." She would protest that she loved her boy and dare anyone to think otherwise.

The pattern went on for years. The mother and the stepfather would act in ways that were hurtful to the son, only to turn around and say that they loved him and wanted only the best for him. They insisted that they were perfect when they weren't. They were like Marie in that regard.

At those times, the son was forced into making one of two decisions at the unconscious level: he had to either discount his parents and their love, or he had to discount himself. He chose the latter option. He discounted himself and he became more troubled.

Later, when Dennis began to challenge the parents' double messages, the mother would appear to agree, only to turn around and disavow her responsibility. She would say, "Yes, I can see how what I said could be interpreted the way you are saying. But . . ." And her "yes . . . but" pattern of communication had the effect of saying, "I know I'm wrong, but really I'm right." "I know I make mistakes, but really they're not mistakes at all." "I know I'm not perfect, but really I am."

Very soon it became apparent that neither the mother nor the stepfather were going to change. At that point, Dennis turned his attention and support to the son.

In individual therapy, the son quickly came to see the bind he was in. But ironically, he went on to subscribe to the perfect-parent myth, too. The whole situation was his parents' fault. If they would only change, he could get better. Parenting was at the root of his problem, and in his view it was a one-way street; in no way was he responsible for the condition he was in.

Only later, after months of therapy, was this young man able to "own" his problem and understand he had to live with the cards he was dealt. He was now responsible for his life and the direction it took, and he had to lay aside blaming and take responsibility for the here and now.

Fortunately, he did receive the help he needed and he got on with the task of becoming a productive and happy person. He eventually took a job and lived life one day at a time. His relationship with his mother and stepfather remained severely strained, but for the most part he was able to cope with their double messages.

What all this leads back to is simply that parental perfection is a myth. We may get depressed or pretend, but the facts don't change: *we aren't perfect persons; therefore we can't be perfect parents.* And so we need to own our own mistakes when they happen, but not own more than what is ours. And we need to teach our children by example to do likewise.

Learning How to Be "Good Enough"

The concept of "good enough," suggested by the psychologist Donald Winnicott, is a very liberating one. It involves accepting "what is" rather than constantly focusing on "what was" or "what ought to be."

The fact is that, as parents, we all make mistakes. Our motives are not completely pure and it doesn't help to pretend that they are.

An interesting phenomenon occurs when we learn to admit our mistakes as parents. If we can do this, our children are more likely to accept us for who and what we are—real people. In turn, they will more than likely be able to accept themselves as they are.

For Christians, this involves recognizing the differences among the four approaches to our mistakes: resistance, sorrow, defeat, and repentance.

Resistance is the position taken by Marie and the mother in the story above. It is fundamentally a defensive position. It places the blame on someone else's shoulders. It is a state of unrepentance.

Sorrow is the position taken by the person who is sorry for his or her mistakes. A sorrowful person can shed buckets of tears, all of them sincere, yet make no commitment to change. Sorrow is merely the admission of an internal feeling state. "I feel bad that I'm wrong, (but I don't really plan to change the way I live or relate to you)."

Defeat is the position taken by our friend Norma. It is the position that says, "I'm wrong, and nothing can be done about it. You'll have to take me the way I am, because that's just the way it is. Really, there is no hope."

Repentance is the position that says "I'm wrong, period. I really have no excuses. I feel bad that you've been hurt by what has happened, and I accept your right to be hurt, angry, or whatever else you may feel." It sheds defensiveness and accepts responsibility for whatever has happened.

Repentance doesn't stop at shouldering responsibility, however. It also moves forward in a hope that is rooted firmly in the grace of God: "As God gives me the grace, I intend to change the way I live and relate to you." In order to be complete, repentance always involves a behavioral change. It includes the decision to do something differently and the action to follow up the decision.

Repentance is rooted firmly in forgiveness as well as hope. "I have asked God's forgiveness. And because of my relationship with Jesus Christ as Savior, I believe he has forgiven me, even though I don't necessarily feel forgiven. Now I ask your forgiveness."

Even though repentance asks forgiveness, it is never manipulative. It says, "I wish as much as is possible that you would forgive me, but you can take as much time as you need, even to the point of never forgiving. My repentance does not demand that you forgive. That's up to you."

Last of all, repentance is ultimately realistic: "Now I must get on with life." Repentance frees us to move on and to put the past behind us.

The essence or heart of the concept of "good enough" is rooted in the idea of repentance and forgiveness—both God's forgiveness and our own. It focuses primarily upon "what is," not only upon "what was" or "what ought to be."

Suggestions for a "Good Enough" Family

Here are four practical suggestions for making a "good enough" family work in real life. As you read, you'll probably think of others you would add to the list.

The first suggestion is: *being a spouse comes before and after being a parent.* We've said this before. It's easy to get totally caught up in the demands of a career, whether that career is in the world of work outside the home or in the world of home and children. The marriage existed before the kids came and (we hope!) will exist after they leave. When they do leave, what will be left?

A couple should never forget that it's the relationship that made the children and it's the relationship that helps them grow. It is too easy to neglect our marriages by paying attention only to the exigencies of house, bills, carpooling— all the myriad of issues that clamor for our attention. If we let it, everything can come before the marriage. But when that happens, the relationship will suffer—and that will be everyone's loss.

Children will almost always try to compete with the

marriage relationship for attention, but they will ultimately be saddened if they win.

Children today grow up with the ever-present fact of divorce. Everywhere they turn it's there. They live with the knowledge that it could happen to their parents, and they dread it. As a result, they have a vested interest in keeping their parents' marriage fresh and alive.

It is natural for children to compete for attention. All human beings start out self-centered and must learn to defer their interests to others.

The thing parents must remember is that children have a vested interest in the stability and vitality of their parents' marriage. They may not know it, but ultimately they *want* Mom and Dad to want each other.

So parents shouldn't be afraid to spend time alone together, to get away and to leave the kids with someone else. It's tough to enjoy one another fully as a married couple when there is always an audience present (or lurking in the next room)!

Our second suggestion is to *focus on creating more good memories than bad ones*. As parents we're memory makers, and it's impossible to create a world for our children in which there are only good memories. If we shackle ourselves to that expectation, we can only fail.

There will inevitably be bad things our children remember about their early lives. Families have to move, pets die, injuries and illnesses happen. We can't and shouldn't protect them from the real world.

The goal to shoot for, then, is for the good memories to outnumber the bad ones when our children are grown. If the good memories predominate, the bad ones will tend to fade, both in their memory and in significance. On the other hand, if the bad ones outnumber the good ones, the kids will tend to remember the bad ones to the exclusion of the good ones and the hurts will persist. It is a creative process, involving everyone's involvement to achieve the end result—hearts and minds filled with more good memories than bad.

Our third suggestion logically follows: *whoever can, provides whatever is needed.* Healthy families are flexible and adaptable. They are not rigid and inflexible.

As we mentioned in chapter 6 the roles in the family should not be absolutely fixed along gender lines, and this is true of generational lines as well. While women may do some things more than men and parents do some things more than children (and vice versa), in healthy families people don't stand around waiting for a job to get done or a responsibility to be taken. If the field needs plowing, do it. If the beans need stirring, stir them. Taking the initiative is more important than being taken care of.

This means that generational lines will sometimes be blurred. Sometimes it may be appropriate for the young to give care to the old, or for the parents to listen to and follow the lead of their children. Real life doesn't always fall into neat and tidy folds and creases. Life sometimes gets wrinkled. And when it does, whoever can should take the iron in hand and do what needs to be done.

A corollary of this is an idea which may ruffle some feathers: *spiritually, it's time to get off Dad's back.* We have come to believe that all the talk about "headship" in Christian families has obscured a vital point: What is important is that *somebody* take on spiritual leadership in the family.

In many if not most families, it is the woman who yearns for spiritual growth in the family. Even in clergy families, including our own, the wife and mother is often more sensitive to the voice of God than is the husband and father.

We don't believe there is a conflict between this idea and the concept of spiritual headship. What we are suggesting is a differentiation between the concepts of leadership and headship. According to our understanding of headship in a family, the biblical position of the husband and father has to do not with who rules, but with who serves. Following the example of Jesus, the head of the family has the greater responsibility to serve. It is the lesson Jesus taught when he washed the disciples' feet in the Upper Room (John 13:3–17).

Leadership, on the other hand, has to do with who is most able. Spiritually, what's important is not whose voice is doing the teaching or the leading; it's the harmony between the singers. Whoever is best at it should lead, and whoever isn't should follow. If interest and ability are more or less even, the partners should take turns. Less conflict will result in more growth. It's just another application of "whoever can does whatever's needed."

Finally, our fourth suggestion for a "good enough" family is that *good parenting self-destructs*. Good parents work themselves out of a job. Parenting has implicit within it a dimension of control and direction, and the idea is to get to the place where parents relate to adult sons and daughters not as controllers but as adult friends, each responsible for their own lives with each other and before God.

Remember, nobody's perfect—parents or children. But the good news is that we're not expected to be perfect. When it comes to living in families, good enough really is good enough!

CHAPTER ELEVEN

Holding On and Letting Go

By now the message of our book should be fairly clear: Staying happily married is tougher than it appears on the surface. There's a lot more that goes into being a mature husband or wife than meets the eye. When you add the dimension of being genuinely Christian in that marriage, the task is doubly difficult—although not impossible, and certainly worthwhile.

In this chapter, we carry our exploration one step further. As we hinted earlier, certain "family styles" in our family of origin (the family in which we grew up) can complicate the work of being married. These family styles affect how a family copes with three major tasks: attachment, separation, and loss. In this chapter we will define the tasks and then describe how four different types of families handle the issues central to those tasks.

As is true of most types, few families will fit the patterns exactly. But we hope our explanation will help you understand some things that went on in your family of origin and also understand more about what is happening in your own marriage and family.

Three Essential Tasks

Becoming One

Any relationship that is to become permanent starts with the process of *attachment*. In chapter 2, we referred to this as a process that begins with bonding and nurture, involves communication and conflict management, and ends with, or yields, mutuality or commitment. At the time it occurs, attachment feels like it will and should last forever. Whether it is a marriage or the birth of a child, the attachment is deep and is meant to be enduring.

In order to be healthy, every relationship must possess the quality of freedom while at the same time possessing the quality of permanence. Attachment refers to that permanent quality in a relationship.

Every family has an "attachment style," which is the way in which the family communicates its commitment to its members. For some families, that style is quiet and muted; the attachment is communicated with a nod of the head, a brief hug, or even a shrug of the shoulders. For other families the attachment is more open and demonstrative. It involves much kissing, hugging, and other public expressions of affection. Both of these families demonstrate attachment, but their modes of expressing it are very different. The key to determining a family's attachment style is to ask, If someone belonged and was accepted in your family, how would they know?

Attachment is at the heart of many of the mother-in-law jokes we sometimes laugh at. And it is at the heart of why so many of us don't feel accepted by our spouse's family—why being an in-law makes us feel like we're an outlaw. When our spouse's family has attached to one another but not to us, we end up feeling as if we're on the outside looking in.

Where this fits in terms of marriage seems fairly obvious. The attachment style of our family of origin has a lot to do with the attachment style of our marriage. And the attachment style of our marriage deeply affects the quality of our relationship together as a married couple.

Where this fits in terms of parenting is that when our ability to bond with one another as a couple is deficient, for whatever reason, we often turn to our children as an alternate source of closeness and togetherness. This places a terrible burden on the parent-child relationship and can lead eventually to its own set of problems.

Letting Go

A relationship that begins with attachment must allow for the reality of *separation* as well. The ultimate separation, of course, is the reality of death, whether it is our own or that of someone we love. Death is a fact that every person and every marriage must eventually face.

However, separation also has a broader meaning. It involves the necessary letting go that must occur at some point in any relationship.

In the marital relationship, separation involves trusting our spouse to be loyal to us and not become involved in an extramarital affair. That is to say that the issue of letting go accounts for much of what is labeled jealousy in marital relationships. This issue also accounts for the inordinate amount of distance that may be needed and demanded by one spouse. And as with attachment, how letting go is handled in our families of origin plays a definite role in how we handle these issues in our own marriage.

The letting go can be very subtle when it comes to

parenting. It may involve a mother's letting her child go to kindergarten for the first day or ride a tricycle around the corner alone. It may involve a father's allowing his teenage son to drive the car for the first time without an adult in the front seat. Or it may involve a child's leaving for college in some distant city.

Separation is both normal and necessary, but it's rarely easy.

Marriages and families have a "separation style" as well as an attachment style. When it came time to grow up and become a person on your own, was the growing up blessed or was it cursed? Was your ongoing development celebrated with appropriate rites of passage? Did the people in your family rejoice in your growth or did they resist it? Did you feel free to grow up and become your own person or did you have to wrench yourself free?

Probably the most important separation issue in a family is the launching of a young person from adolescence into adulthood.

This issue is central for those of us who are married because how our families handled the task of separation has a lot to do with whether or not we really were free to "leave father and mother and become one flesh" with our spouse. Some families hold on by using guilt and their offsprings' sense of obligation to manipulate them. The bond is so tight that the new couple is never truly free to establish their own sense of family identity.

Other families don't hold on enough; they push their young out the door before they're ready. The message for their offspring is to leave the nest and not come back, regardless of whether they're ready to fly. Somewhere between these two extremes is the balance we all need.

Handling Loss

The third task, following attachment and separation, is the task of *handling loss*. What we suggest is that for every separation, be it big or small, there is a concomitant sense of loss. And for every loss, there is an accompanying grief.

Grief is an interesting emotion. Though it is pervasive and a part of everyone's life, it is often pushed away and denied. We all understand the relationship between grief and death. What we don't seem to understand is the relationship between grief and other kinds of loss.

For example, whereas grief is considered acceptable when someone dies, it's not considered acceptable at a wedding. Why? Because the event is supposed to be a time of celebration. But a wedding also involves some loss, and some elements of grief.

Maybe we're more aware of this kind of grief because of the wedding of our daughter Sheryl this past year. Looking back, it was a time of celebration, but a time of curious sadness as well.

At the moment when it was time for Lucy to walk down the aisle as the mother of the bride she was ready to burst into tears. "Dear God, I'm going to blubber like a baby," she thought. At the same time, Sheryl whispered to Dennis, "Oh Daddy. I think I'm going to cry." Dennis, who had just been thinking the same thing himself, took a deep breath and reassured her that everything was going to be all right. As they walked to the front of the congregation, the bridegroom, Jaime, met the two of them. And he *did* begin to cry.

There we stood. On a day of joy and celebration we all were close to tears, if not swimming in them. How could that be? Partly, of course, the tears reflected all our strong emotions. But they also involved some grief.

A wedding does, in fact, involve a loss. The creation of a new relationship does not annul the effect of the change in the other relationships. Our family was being changed, and so was Jaime's. Though the day was a joyous one, our loss was real just the same.

Shannon, our youngest daughter, had broached this issue of loss years earlier, when Sheryl was preparing to leave for college. "When Sheryl leaves," she asked, "will we still be a family?" "Yes," we answered, even though we had not yet coped with the meaning of her leaving. But if Shannon had asked on the day of Sheryl's wedding, "Now that Sheryl is married, will the family be the same?" we would have had to answer, "No, but we'll still be a family."

However, not every loss in families is experienced as grief. Sometimes, rather than experience the loss and subsequent grief, families experience the separation with anger. They deal with their loss by becoming *mad rather than sad*. The paradox is that, instead of facing their feelings of loss and communicating them appropriately, they fill their lives with conflict and bitterness, thus forcing a separation. The son who yells and screams at his parents because they won't let him be free (that usually means "no rules") storms off into a "far country," saying to himself that the reason he left is that he hates them and they hate him. Often the opposite is true: there is too much closeness, and the only way he can break free is to create a kind of centrifugal force, energized by anger, that flings the adolescent far into the night.

Another example can be found in the way Lucy coped with a move several years ago. Dennis had begun working at the seminary where we both presently serve. The commute on Los Angeles freeways, even in the best of traffic, took an hour each way. After two years of this, we made a mutual decision to move closer to the school.

When the time came to move, however, Lucy was furious. On the day the moving van came, Dennis was elsewhere on some sort of speaking engagement. (That's the way he often copes. He leaves.) He was supposed to arrive at the new house just in time to supervise the movers as they unpacked the van. As is often the case, things didn't work out as he planned and the move itself was left totally in Lucy's hands. She coped wonderfully with the pressures of dealing with the movers, but later her wrath towards Dennis boiled over.

Initially, the fight was over his irresponsibility in managing the move. In that sense her anger was appropriate. But the feelings outlived the facts. She stayed mad for weeks—long past the point that her anger was appropriate.

Months and many tears later, Lucy was able to understand what the problem really was. Wherever she lives, she immediately puts down deep roots, and she had lived in Orange County for nine years. For Lucy, the move from North Orange County to Pasadena was more than a mere geographical change; it was a wrenching loss of friends and familiar surroundings. Lucy needed to grieve over her loss. Instead, she got mad. When she was finally able to let herself feel the sadness, she was able to accept the loss and to get on with her life.

The fact is that much anger between couples and in families is actually masked grief over a loss or series of losses that have never been worked through.

Another point is worth making here: *Everyone's loss is the worst.* In the face of loss and accompanying grief, the tendency is to minimize the grief by casting it into some kind of hierarchy—deciding which losses are major and which are minor. Whether it is a child's grief over the death of a hamster or a spouse's grief over the loss of a job, loss is loss and grief is grief. And comfort comes when loss is shared and not denied.

A marriage, a move, a child's graduation from high school, a chronic illness, the death of a parent—all involve significant loss and the need for comfort. Supposedly lesser losses provoke grief as well. A daughter's loss of a boyfriend, the death of a pet cat, a spouse's promotion that doesn't come through—these too involve loss, and those who have suffered the loss deserve to be comforted. Telling those who grieve that the situation could be worse rarely helps because, at the time, their grief *is* the worst. Sharing their grief is the best comfort that could be offered. And many times, no one can comfort us better than the person who is closest to us—husband or wife.

What Type of Family Are You?

Having discussed the major tasks of attachment, separation and loss, we now turn to four kinds of marriages and families that handle these tasks differently. They are listed in an order that suggests a continuum ranging from unhealthy to healthy. Our intent is not to pigeonhole anyone, only to suggest the ways in which people typically cope with these major tasks.*

It's important to remember here that marriages and families change, depending upon their "seasons" of life. Accordingly, a family may be one type early in the marriage and another later on. The issue of greater importance is not necessarily the stage you're in, but the direction you're moving.

Once again, the nature of a "type"—whatever it may be—is that it is generally descriptive and not absolute. The use of types is intended to be useful, not predictive; they certainly aren't set in cement.

As you read the following descriptions, think of the kind of family you grew up in. How did they handle attachment, separation, and loss? What was their style? And, ask yourself about the marriage and family you're living in and creating now.

The "Super Glue"® Family

Super Glue® is a strange substance. When it sticks, it sticks, and whatever it bonds stays bonded. In effect, the line that separates one piece from the other disappears, and the two pieces, once distinct, are now one.

Some marriages and families are so closely bonded it's as if they are permanently attached with Super Glue®.

Attachment in a Super-Glue® family is a life-or-death matter. It's as if one or all of the members would die if there were to be separation. Because of the strength of the bond, any attempt to establish one's own identity is blocked.

The message between the married partners or between

*We are thankful for the contributions John Bowlby (author of the three books, *Attachment, Separation,* and *Loss*) and Charles Gerkin (author of *Crisis Experience in Modern Life*) have made to our thinking about these issues.

the parents and the children is, "I cannot live without you and you cannot live without me." Although the words may never be actually spoken, the message is communicated just the same.

In Super-Glue® marriages, the individuals in the relationship are not allowed to have thoughts, ideas, or time and space of their own. Being a separate person is interpreted as violating the "two shall become one flesh" principle.

In Super-Glue® families, the parents want to know not only what their child is doing, but also what their child is thinking and feeling. They think as if they're one person, and act as if what's going on inside the child is going on simultaneously in the parent(s).

Children of Super-Glue® families learn to believe that the world is a hostile place. They are raised to feel they are not safe beyond the eyesight and earshot of the parents.

When those children grow up and marry, often the glue that holds their family of origin together demands that there be daily telephone contact and multiple visits between the newlyweds and the parents. Everything that the spouse thinks or feels must be shared. There are no secrets. There is no privacy. There are no separate lives. There is no opportunity for the marriage to develop a life of its own.

Often at this point the issue of safety is turned upside down, and the grown children are inordinately worried about and feel responsible for their parents' health and happiness. As one of Dennis's clients said about her mother, "If she dies, I think I will die with her. There would be no reason to go on living."

An example of a Super-Glue® marriage would be the relationship between Davy and Sheldon Vanaucken as described in Sheldon's bestseller, *A Severe Mercy*. Vanaucken describes his marriage to his wife, Davy. Their goal was to so bury their individual selves in the relationship that there would be no place for others. Their interests, their work, their very lives were so intertwined that whoever they might be as individuals was lost. So when Davy died, it was as if Sheldon died too. It took him years to deal with what was essentially an unhealthy closeness.

In commenting later on this relationship, Vanaucken's friend C. S. Lewis noted that the Vanauckens' love had been so intense that it took on the form of idolatry. Such is often the case with attachment in a Super-Glue® marriage or family.

Separation in a Super-Glue® family is marked by either rebellion or panic. Even the shortest leave-taking is like tearing the heart out of one or the other of the members. As a result, relationships are characterized by constant tension. Sometimes the tension will manifest itself in a psychosomatic illness, or in the case of children, in running away, or in an eating disorder. In children of such families, school phobias are also common.

The underlying factor in all these disorders is the belief, reinforced by any or all of the individuals in the family, that the marriage, either spouse, or the child "will die" without the presence of the others.

In a Super-Glue® marriage, the reaction of panic may manifest itself in different ways. A woman's obsession with the death of her husband, for example, may be the residual effect of her panicky Super-Glue® parent/child relationship. In other Super-Glue® marriages, one of the partners may be overly dependent, unable to drive the car, cook a meal, or do anything for themselves. The panicky partner is lost without the other and almost will not go out on their own.

Whatever the symptoms, the result is that one or both of the partners feel smothered and boxed in. They cry out for room, for freedom to be themselves, and for freedom from being responsible for the life and happiness of their spouse.

The issue of loss and grief in a Super-Glue® family is marked by denial; they refuse to accept loss as a part of life. They are forever focused on the past, and their intent is to keep things the way they always have been. As a result, feelings often run deep, and they often run over.

It is not unusual in a Super-Glue® marriage or family for transition time to become chaotic and emotionally explosive.

Because they deny that there is a loss, there is nowhere for the grief to go so it becomes a volatile issue.

An example of a typical Super-Glue® family might be helpful at this point. Suppose the family is Christian and consists of a mother, a father, and three kids. The eldest child is seventeen, a boy, and a senior in high school. The teenage years have been rocky, but the family members have all more or less coped. Now they are faced with a significant decision: Where will the son go to college and where will he live?

If the attachment and separation issues are still unresolved (and we would expect them to be), the thought of the boy's leaving home provokes all kinds of fears and anxieties both in his parents and in the boy himself. But the essence of their feelings is that they want him close and he wants to go far away. After much arguing and verbal pushing and shoving, it is decided that the parents will only support him if he goes to a "safe" Christian college nearby. That way, they don't have to worry about his getting into trouble. The school will play the role of his parents away from home.

Down deep inside, the mother really wants the boy to go to college nearby so that he can be home more. The father wants him close by because he knows that otherwise the mother will fret night and day and that he, the father, will have to fill the hole in the mother's life created by the son's leaving.

As the time for the son to leave draws nearer, a big fight occurs. Ostensibly it's over whether or not the son should live at home or live in the dorms. "He could commute," the mother says. "Commuting will cost less money," says the father. "But it won't feel like I'm at college if I have to live at home," says the son. Finally, it's decided that he should give dorm living a try and that they'll reevaluate the situation at the end of the first semester.

The first few months that the son is away are terrible! The son does poorly in his classes and seems to be depressed and lethargic. He skips classes and sleeps through two or three tests.

At home, the mother is constantly on the verge of tears and experiences severe menstrual problems, which are diagnosed by her gynecologist as the early onset of menopause. The father is constantly sniping at the boy on weekends about how much money he's costing the family.

By the middle of the semester, the father becomes aware of a situation at work that might possibly result in his losing his job. His blood pressure soars.

At Christmas break, the son returns home and announces that college "just isn't for me." He says he's going to get a job at a nearby fast-food restaurant, live at home, and "think about" joining the army at some point in the future. (He's very vague about this).

Mom's depression lifts and Dad is relieved about the money, but the son has cycled back into the family feeling badly about himself because he "failed" in college.

The Super-Glue® family defeats any attempt of any member to become a person functioning beyond the boundaries of the family system. Attachment and separation are cast in life or death terms, and loss and grief are denied or put off until another day—or at least until the next child is ready to leave home!

The "Static Cling" Family

Sometimes when clothes come out of our dryer at home, they cling together because of static electricity. The socks cling to the towels as if they were meant to be attached. When you separate the pieces, the laundry room snaps and crackles with the sound of the garments releasing each other. Some marriages and families also cling to and clutch one another, not in the more absolute sense of the Super-Glue® family, but in the sense of holding on to one another and resisting separation.

Attachment in a static-cling family is similar to the symbiosis of the Super-Glue® family, but is not as extreme. They need one another, not in the sense of staying alive, but in the sense of being happy. One won't "die" without the other, but they probably won't be satisfied or content without each other.

According to Charles Gerkin, in the static-cling family (or "mutually dependent" in his terminology) the traditional mother typically creates a relationship with her children in which the children both depend on her and constantly take her for granted. Her feelings are often hurt. Nobody appreciates her effort or her sacrifices.

The traditional father in such a family buys his children's affection with gifts and/or permissiveness. He's usually the "good-guy" and Mom's the "bad guy." The kids soon learn that they can work the parents against one another, and that the one whose side you want to stay on is Dad's!

Attachment in a static-cling marriage is often marked by the child-centeredness of the relationship. The parents are so accustomed to giving to their children that they neglect their own relationship. They struggle with intimacy because they have never worked at it; they've been too busy with other things. When they are alone together, they feel like strangers. They have memories of past closeness but have trouble translating that closeness into a present reality.

Separation in a static-cling family is marked by what Gerkin calls "reluctant autonomy." None of the kids really wants to leave home. When they do, they ache to come back. Growing up has no real attraction, because who could ever find a better deal than they have at home? The food's good, the rent's great. Staying an adolescent becomes a lifestyle to be held on to as long as you can get away with it.

A static-cling marriage is often typified by a kind of "stuckness" when it comes to separation. Neither of the parents has ever become a person in his or her own right, and both are fearful of trying. To them, the safe place is the home, where they are needed by the children. The tragedy looming over the horizon is the probability that the children will eventually leave home. Somehow the message that is communicated is: "Don't leave. We need you in order to feel good about ourselves. If you leave, so will the meaning in our lives. So stay."

Whereas loss and grief in a Super-Glue® family bring on denial and helplessness, the issue of *loss and grief in a static-cling family* is marked by resistance—especially to new relationships that are perceived as threatening loss. Somehow these new relationships are blocked because the newcomers are seen as intruders. The marriage and family are to be protected from "outsiders." (Being "unequally yoked" takes on broad meanings here indeed.)

The static-cling marriage is characterized by covert rather than overt dependency. Typically, communication between the spouses takes on a pattern of defensiveness and blaming. They are always trying to figure out whose fault it is if something goes wrong. Though they are not suffocating each other, as in the Super-Glue® marriage, the partners can easily feel lost because new things, new places, new ideas, and new friends seem threatening. Growth is scary and development is foreboding.

Suppose our hypothetical mom, dad, and three kids family were a static-cling family instead of a Super-Glue® family. What would they be like?

In the first place, when it came time for the eldest son to graduate from high school, it probably wouldn't occur to him to go anywhere other than the local college, where he could still live at home. Probably the reason given would be in order to "keep his job," which may be true in part, but a more significant reason would be that he just doesn't want to live on his own.

Classes begin in the fall, and he does pretty well. However, Mom is resentful because he's eighteen years old and still expects her not only to wash his laundry, but also to pick up his room. It never occurs to her to expect the kids to take care of themselves—after all, she's the mother, isn't she?

Dad is affectionately known as "deep pockets." He vicariously participates in his son's freedom by financing the expensive ski weekends in the local mountains. When the insurance rates on the car go out of sight because of the son's tickets, the father simply reaches deeper and makes up the difference (after an appropriate "man-to-man talk" with his son).

Several years later, the parents wake up one morning and realize that their three children are still living at home and that they have never taken a vacation by themselves (and still can't) because they can't afford it. Their relationship as a couple has suffered and they feel they don't know each other very well. When they total up the trips their kids have taken and the places they have been, the parents feel cheated, even though they know, somehow, that they were a part of the pattern that had been created.

Down deep inside, the parents fear that, even if their kids leave, eventually the kids will move home again and the cycle will never change. They had a marriage before the children came into their lives, and they wonder if they will ever have the opportunity to be a couple on their own again. But at the same time, they just can't bring themselves to "hurt" their kids by saying no to them.

The "Tug-of-War" Family

The third type of family is the family that is characterized by constant power struggles. Typically, this kind of marriage or family casts their relationships into a dominance/submission framework. The "chain-of-command," so important to how they function as a married couple or as a family, often becomes the rope in a prolonged tug-of-war between various family members.

Attachment in a tug-of-war family equates bonding with control. Being loved and being submitted to are thought of as synonymous. Who's in charge becomes the measure of caring and concern. As a result, there are constant authority struggles, conflict over friends, hours, limits.

Attachment in a tug-of-war marriage is fraught with tension over power issues. Responsibility and authority are often separated. The male is the "head of the house" and therefore has the authority. The female is responsible for how it runs. In a curious way, in their relationship compliance is traded for closeness. The household can all run smoothly if everyone cooperates. The problem is that most marriages and families don't run that smoothly.

Separation in a tug-of-war family centers upon the "if only" game. If only the parents would treat the teenager fairly, then he or she would quit the destructive behavior. If only they wouldn't nag, then he or she would be responsible.

Married couples play the "if only" game too. "I'd help more around the house, if only she didn't nag me all of the time." "If only he'd be a 'real' man, then I'd be more interested sexually." The tug-of-war marriage is characterized by hassles over who's in charge, who's right and who's wrong. Eventually the relationship becomes a place of weariness rather than respite, something to avoid rather than to embrace.

The issue of *loss and grief in the tug-of-war family* and marriage is characterized by one word: negativity. They don't know how to let go without being angry. They mask their grief with quarrels and fighting. They know how to be mad; they don't know how to be sad.

If our fictional family were a tug-of-war family, when it came time for the eldest son to leave home, the parents (the father in particular) probably would say, "good riddance." The relationship between father and son has been one struggle after another for years. Quarrels over grades, drugs, and the boy's choice of friends have been eroding the relationship between the father and his son ever since the boy hit his teens.

For years, the mother has lived her life caught between the father and the son. She has cried, she has coddled, and she has coerced, but nothing has worked. Now as the time approaches, the eighteenth birthday seems like a magic date. She looks forward to the event if only so that the tension in the house will be reduced.

The son is counting the days, too. He can't wait. All of

their nagging and complaining will be behind him, and he'll be on his own. Never mind that he doesn't have a job; he can always stay with friends and something will "turn up." He and his friends sit around, some smoking dope, fantasizing how they're going to make a killing as rock musicians. Someone will discover them just like the Rolling Stones were discovered.

After he graduates, the son comes home one night to find his clothes and stereo packed and waiting on the front steps. He throws his worldly goods into his car and drives over to a friend's apartment, muttering under his breath that he'll "show them."

Sometimes the couple breathes a sigh of relief. Many times, however, the focus of the conflict merely shifts, and conflict becomes a permanent part of the marital relationship as a steady-state. For some reason, the family seems to need some kind of conflict in order to stay alive. Such a marriage is sometimes described as being "conflict-habituated."

The "Post-It®" Family

The fourth and most healthy family type is like the little notes, made by the 3M company, that stick on the refrigerator door in the kitchen. These little notes have the remarkable ability to stick to something, release their hold, and then stick again. We have learned to use them for most every kind of communication. They are used as bookmarks, as reminders, and for various and sundry other purposes—all because they have the ability to attach without binding and to let go without losing their stickiness.

Attachment in a Post-It® family and marriage is welcomed because it doesn't mean giving up personal individuality. The individuality of each individual is both welcomed and nurtured. The mystery is that at the same time, the members of the family are free to belong to one another without getting lost in the process.

A Post-It® marriage is an enigma to some. Somehow the

married partners are able to negotiate their relationship in such a way as to allow for their freedom as persons without negatively impinging upon the marriage. They recognize the need for interdependence. They have the freedom to be autonomous persons in their own right, but they choose to limit their freedom for the sake of their spouse or their relationship. And when they do this, they don't feel cheated.

Early on in the relationship between the parents and the children of a Post-It® family, a kind of mutuality begins to form. Respect characterizes their commitment to one another, all within the boundaries of love and control.

Separation in a Post-It® family is marked by a process of negotiated freedom. Freedom and responsibility go hand in hand. They are not granted automatically; they are earned. There is a constant restructuring of the "house rules" depending upon the development and performance of the family members.

Expectations are explicit and are tailored to the abilities of each person. They are not determined by some vague or pervasive norm set by others, characterized by statements such as "All the other kids can go. Why can't I?" or "I don't care. I just don't want you to do that. We don't act that way." Rules have reasons and it's appropriate to state the reasons and to expect them to be followed. However, enforcement of rules is flexible enough to allow changes or exceptions when circumstances warrant it. In our experience, this is the characteristic of "reasonableness" mentioned by James in his Epistle and discussed in chapter 8. It means to be open to reason, to be willing to be persuaded if you are wrong.

Separation in a Post-It® marriage is approached in a way that is rare in today's world. The attitude is that the marriage partners are both free to become all that God intends them to be—always, however, within the bounds of their relationship.

Rather than being rigidly equal, they emphasize equity. Equality sometimes breeds fixed equilibrium or static balance in a relationship rather than a dynamic growth. Equity, on the other hand, connotes a "your turn . . . my turn" kind of relationship. *Post-It® partners are radically committed to one another's growth as persons and are willing to make the sacrifices necessary for that growth to be accomplished.* It's virtually impossible for life to be lived as equals if there isn't equity.

The understanding between these partners is that the kind of person an individual feels called to be is up to that individual, but that the choice must be made within the boundaries of the choices that have already been made. In that sense, making choices involves a mutual submission on the part of both marriage partners rather than a unidirectional submission of one spouse to the other.

Separation in a Post-It® marriage probably includes another unusual characteristic for a marriage: the freedom for each partner to have personal friends of both sexes. This goes for interests as well; being "one" is not considered identical with being the same; the assumption is that the spouses are allowed to have separate friends and interests.

Obviously, trust becomes an absolutely necessary quality of such a relationship, because if you can't trust each other, neither of you can really be free. And if you're not free, you can't really choose to be interdependent.

Communication in a Post-It® marriage comes to mean times of meaningful intersection between two people who are individuals in their own right but who share a close commitment with their spouse. As a result, they probably have to fight to protect their times together because their world—whether it involves the children, a career, or an avocation—can consume them if they let it. Times of communication are times to be cherished and valued as times of sharing and openness. Their marriage is a place where they can be themselves without pretense.

The issue of *loss and grief in a Post-It® family* involves a healthy sense that the past, present, and future fit together into an integrated whole. Because they can trust God for their future, they can let go of their past when it comes time. Rather than resist their grief or deny it, they are able to embrace their feelings as appropriate and beneficial.

When change comes, members of a Post-It® family can feel good about that change because they have learned to trust the process of growth in each other and have come to want the best for one another. Rather than being seen as antithetical to happiness, life, loss and grief are experienced as being a natural and fitting part of life. The idea is that the seed that falls into the ground must die in order for there to be life, and that this principle is true of people as well. It is right that the young grow up and go away. And it is right that the young grow old and face the end of their physical life on earth.

If our hypothetical family is a Post-It® family, when it comes time for the eldest son to leave home, everyone is aware that there have been many departures before. Early in his life, the son experienced his parents' support in trying his wings; for instance, he worked away from home one summer during high school and came home a wiser and better person. Everyone expects that when he leaves, Mother will cry. She always does. Maybe the son will cry and maybe Dad will. But everything will be OK.

The family talked about the son's college for years, and it has always been taken for granted that he would choose the school best suited to his goals—and also that he would be responsible for some of his college expenses. He didn't get the scholarship he had hoped for but that's OK too. He's aware that his parents, though sad about his leaving, are happy for him, and also happy for themselves because his departure means that his younger siblings will not be far behind him. The parents are prepared for an empty nest.

He knows that even after he leaves, his mom and dad will always be there for him. He will always be their son. The difference is that he is no longer their *child*. They remain father and son, mother and son, but will also be friends.

Trusting God for Your Real Marriage

We've seen four types of marriages and families, each trying to accomplish the tasks of attachment, separation, and loss. The important question is not where you find yourself or your family at any given moment; it's the direction you are moving. The great hope of the Christian is that God is as concerned as we are with our growth as individuals, as married couples, and as families.

In the Old Testament, the marvelous example of Job is a fitting example of what it is that we are trying to say. It was Job who said, "Man that is born of a woman is of few days, and full of trouble. He comes forth like a flower, and withers; he flees like a shadow, and continues not" (Job 14:1–2).

When Job spoke those words, he was buffeted from all sides. He had lost family and fortune. His wife had turned against him. Even his friends were questioning the very essence of his being, his relationship with God. Time after time, his critics questioned his integrity, always under the guise of bringing comfort. Time after time he answered them. He acknowledged his frustration and despair. The words he spoke were words of anguish.

Yet, when Job looked back over his life as a whole, he was able to gain perspective from one fact: he would be raised from the dead. And so he also spoke words of triumph and hope:

> For I know that my Redeemer lives, and at last he will stand upon the earth; and after my skin has been thus destroyed, then from my flesh I shall see God (Job 19:25–26).

Attachment, separation, loss and grief—for men and women, whether in a marriage or in a family or not, this is the necessary pattern of our faith. The rhythm is inevitable and is predictable.

What all of this means in terms of real-life marriage is that what is true for an individual like Job is also true for relationships. Though Job was speaking in an eternal sense, the same pattern, the same rhythm, can be true of our relationships with one another.

Our typical expectation is that we will marry, live our lives until we are old, and then that one of us will bury the other, comforting ourselves with the hope of the resurrection. We assume that death when it comes will come at the right time and with appropriate warning.

The reality is, however, that in the course of every relationship there will be multiple occurrences of the themes of attachment, separation, loss, and grief. It won't happen just once and there may be no warning. Real people may experience the pattern many times.

Life in the sense of bonding and attachment, death in the sense of despair and hopelessness, burial in the sense of loss and grief, and resurrection in the sense of renewal and hope are normal in the course of a marriage.

The reappearance of these themes throughout a relationship is much like a symphony. They weave in and out of the music, creating a drama of counterpoint. The way each theme plays against the other creates the tension within the music; the way the discord dissolves into harmony creates the resolution. The beauty and greatness of the music is its ability to capture the richness of many voices while at the same time preserving the simplicity of single melodies.

Real-life marriage is not a monotonal, simplistic statement containing only a beginning and an end—only birth and resurrection. Like a symphony, it is full and complex and magnificent. Relationships in general, and marriage in particular, if they are to be sustained in real life, must embrace the whole of the cycle. There must be death and burial as well as life and resurrection. Real life demands it all.

The temptation is to cling to life and push death and burial away as vile enemies. But the difficulty when we try to do that is that we lose the continuity of God's grace in our lives. For it is in those times of death and burial that God comes to us and makes himself real. For the Christian in real-life, there is no resurrection without death and burial. And without resurrection there truly is no hope.

Whoever we are, and whatever kind of marriage or family we find ourselves in at the moment, our blessed hope as Christians is the same hope that sustained and motivated Job. Our continued hope is in the reality that even in the midst of real-life difficulties, our God in his grace can—and does—make all things new.

Study Guide

This study guide is designed to be usable for any of several situations. It could be used by a married couple as a tool for better understanding and enriching the marriage relationship. Or it could be used in a couples' group as a basis for discussion and study. Finally, it could be used by a couple who is not yet married as a means of exploring their future relationship and getting to know one another better.

If you are reading this book as a couple, we suggest you first answer the questions separately, then come together and discuss them. (In answering, try to be as honest as you can, but as gentle as possible!) In some of the chapters there are exercises or activities you may want to do together.

If you are in a group with other couples, we suggest that each individual answer the questions, then meet with his/her partner before the group discussion starts. That way, husband and wife can agree what subjects are private and which are "fair game" for group discussion.

If you are using this book as a premarital study, you may have trouble answering those questions that ask about your experiences with your partner—especially if you haven't been together for a long time. You may also find it difficult, in the glow of being in love, to assess your differences realistically. We suggest, when a question doesn't seem to apply, that you answer it with another married couple in mind. In some cases, you may want to think about your own parents' relationship, because it is common for married people to find themselves mimicking their parents' behavior in relationships.

One final word: Proceed slowly. Many of the issues that are the basis for this book are difficult and may stir up deep feelings. If at any point your discussion becomes too much for either of you, call time out and agree to continue your discussion at a later time. If possible, find someone you know and trust with whom you can share some of your feelings and frustrations (not necessarily the issues themselves, which you or your partner may consider private). You may even choose to seek professional help if an issue becomes too rocky. But by all means, do keep trying to communicate with each other about the real-life issues of your real-life marriage.

Chapter 1

1. Try to remember your thoughts and feelings on your wedding day. (You might want actually to get out your wedding pictures—or, if you are meeting in a group, bring your pictures to the group and compare.) What were your expectations about marriage and about your life together? If you are not yet married, make a list of some of the things you expect of your life together. What is most important to you—companionship, good sex, laughing together, etc.?

2. In what ways has your marriage lived up to your expectations? In what ways has it failed to live up to expectations?

3. Try to remember your first big "falling out." What issues were at stake? What was the outcome of the conflict?

4. What are the five kinds of lasting marriages listed in this chapter? Which marriage style (or styles) characterized the home in which you grew up?

5. How would you describe your marriage style right now? (If you are not married, which style most characterizes your relationship?) Have you fallen into different patterns at previous times in your life together?

6. Are you satisfied with your current marriage style? If not, which of the five kinds of marriages described would you want in your own relationship?

7. How do you respond to the idea that we "count the cost" of living in a marriage? Do you find it too negative or difficult? Why or why not?

8. Based on your reading of the chapter, compose a brief (1 or 2 sentence) definition of "real-life marriage." What elements would make it up?

Chapter 2

1. What do you think of when you hear the word *intimacy?* Do you tend to think of it more in terms of passion/desire, sacrifice/duty, or friendship? How do you respond to the chapter's assertion that friendship is the most realistic and helpful model of intimacy?

2. How would you describe the intimacy needs of you and your partner? Are you satisfied with the level of intimacy in your marriage? Do you think your partner needs or wants more or less intimacy than you do?

3. According to the David/Jonathan friendship model described in this chapter, the *robe* in a relationship refers to the couple's shared status. Based on this model, how would you describe your shared "robe" (ornate, plain wool, tattered, etc.)? What would you like it to look like? Is status a problem issue in your marriage? Which of you has the most problem at this point?

4. According to the model, who in your marriage has the *tunic* responsibility—nurturing and care-giving? Is this responsibility equally shared, or does it fall more heavily on one partner? Is this a problem issue in your marriage?

5. What *sword,* or protective device, do you tend to use when the going gets rough in your relationship? What does your partner use? Describe a typical "sword fight" in your relationship.

6. What *bow and arrows*—intimate information used as distancing weapons—do you tend to use in your relationship? What does your spouse use? In your opinion, has the use of bow and arrows created too much distance between you?

7. How do you feel about the idea of vulnerability in marriage? In your opinion, is total vulnerability a healthy circumstance? What are the advantages/disadvantages of vulnerability in a relationship?

8. What are some of the barriers that stand in the way of greater intimacy in your marriage?

Chapter 3

1. What early experiences are you aware of (either remembered or told to you) that could have affected your or your spouse's capacity for intimate relationships—positively or negatively? What can you remember or surmise about the bonding and nurturing each of you experienced?

2. What are the four components of good relational communication listed in this chapter? According to this description, what were the communication strong points and weak points in your family of origin? (For example, did you feel free and able to express thoughts but not feelings? Were you always sure that one parent would hear and respond consistently but not the other?)

3. What are the communication strong and weak points in your relationship today? Is communication a problem for you?

4. Do you tend to approach communication "thought first," "thought only," "feelings only," or "feelings first"? What about your spouse?

5. What are the four kinds of conflict resolution described in this chapter? Which best describes the way conflict was typically handled in your family of origin? Which best describes the way you tend to handle conflict now? Is conflict resolution a problem in your relationship?

Chapter 4

1. After reading the section describing the visual personal map, try to think of someone you know who fits this pattern. Who do you know who is an auditory/tonal? Do you know a kinesthetic? How do you tend to relate to these people?

2. After reading the chapter and filling in the chart p. 68, would you say you are a visual, auditory/tonal, or kinesthetic? Which of the three types is your partner?

3. Try to remember a specific incident in the past where differences in personal maps may have caused conflict or misunderstanding in your relationship. How could understanding your differences have helped ameliorate the problem?

4. Try to recall a specific incident in your life together where the differences in your personal maps complemented one another and helped you as a couple see a situation more accurately?

5. How could you make better use of your differences as a source of enrichment for your marriage?

Chapter 5

1. What are the four sets of "compass points" which, according to this chapter, determine temperament?

2. Use the chart on pp. 82–83 to get an idea of your own temperament. What 4-letter combination do you end up with?

3. Without consulting your partner, do the chart *for* him or her. What 4-letter combination do you come up with for your partner?

4. Compare your self-evaluation with your spouse's evaluation of you. Are there places your assessments differ? Any ideas why? Work together to come to a basic agreement as to what combination applies to each of you.

5. In which of the four categories are you and your spouse most different? In which are you more alike?

6. Which of the four major temperament combinations listed in the chapter best describes you? Your spouse?

7. What are some times in your life together when the differences in your temperament resulted in conflict or tension? How did you resolve this conflict? Could an understanding of temperaments have made a difference in how you handled your conflict?

8. List the three principles mentioned in this chapter for handling differences. If you had to pick just one as your basic guide for dealing with your particular set of differences, which would you pick? Why?

Chapter 6

1. At what three levels does the issue of power in a marriage operate? According to the authors' explanation, where do you think the balance of power lies in your relationship? Is this satisfactory to you?

2. Do you think the term "dual-career couple" applies to you? Why or why not? What term would you prefer?

3. What are the five points of dual-career tension listed in this chapter? Which of these is the most problematic for you? If you are not yet married, or if you are not a dual-career couple, which do you think would potentially pose the biggest problem?

4. What are some of the basic assumptions that, according to the authors, must be challenged in order for a dual-career marriage to work well?

5. In your own words, describe the basic commitment to shared power the authors recommend in this chapter. How would you rephrase that commitment to apply to your own marriage?

6. List the seven principles given in this chapter for managing a dual-career marriage. Which ones are more difficult for you to apply? Which are harder for your spouse?

Chapter 7

1. In your own words, describe the difference between a value and a belief. According to this chapter, which is the more powerful in terms of behavior?

2. Referring to figure 1 on p. 111, write beside each of the following objects a number (positive or negative) that reflects the value you tend to attach to that object. When you are finished, compare your list with that of your partner:

   a. Celebrating birthdays

   b. Continuing your education

   c. Entertaining as a couple

   d. Travel/regular vacations

   e. Having pets

    f. Going to church

    g. Eating meals together

    h. Regular visits/conversations with extended family

    i. Having children

    j. Being successful

    k. Personal attractiveness

    l. A clean house/neatness

3. What are some areas where your values differ from those of your partner? In what areas are your values congruent?

4. Describe a situation in your own life when you found yourself doing something that was contrary to what you believed. According to this chapter, what does this say about your values system?

5. How do you respond to the authors' reinterpretation of Paul's teaching about being "unequally yoked"? Do you agree with this interpretation?

6. What are some issues in your own relationship that may reflect a fundamental difference in values between you?

Chapter 8

1. According to the chapter, which are the three characteristics of a values system based on "wisdom from below"?

2. The authors mention the phrase, "Let's do it to them before they do it to us," as representing an earthly values system. Make a list of other common phrases that can be seen as reflecting "wisdom from below."

3. What four "earthbound attitudes" are listed in this chapter. For each one, try to list an example from your own experience where this attitude caused a problem in relationships (marital or other).

4. Make a list of common activities—your own or others'—that could fall under the general headings of "chaotic" and "worthless," as described in this chapter. Have you ever thought of these behaviors as being based on an earthly value system?

5. List the seven objects of a heavenly values system as described in this chapter. Beside each word, write down the name of a person you know whose behavior shows that he or she values that particular object.

6. For each of the seven objects listed, consider specific ways your behavior and the behavior of your spouse might change as that object became central to the value system of both of you.

Chapter 9

1. Where are you in the family life cycle described in this chapter? In what ways do your experience and/or plans follow the typical cycle described, and in what ways do they differ? How would a difference at one stage (i.e. deciding not to have children) affect the subsequent stages?

2. What are the "twin tasks" that must take place at stage 1 in the family cycle? How have you and your spouse handled (or how are you handling) these tasks? Has either been a problem for you?

3. What are the basic tasks involved in stage 2? How have you handled these issues in your marriage—or how do you propose to handle them?

4. What are some of the reasons children can be hard on a marriage? List some of the specific pressures having children has put on your relationship, then list some of the ways having children has enriched or improved the relationship. (If you have no children, look either at your parents' relationship or that of another couple you know well who have children.)

5. Refer back to chapter 3, which described some of the ways our early experiences influence our capacity for intimacy. These early experiences take place primarily during stages 3 and 4 in the life cycle of our family of origin. How could the pressures of the family life cycle during these years affect bonding, nurture, communication, and conflict resolution in the family?

6. What unique pressures are involved in the school-age years of a marriage? What are the most important parental tasks at this stage?

7. Why is stage 5—adolescence—so difficult for most couples? What are the specific pressures? Describe either what this situation was/is like in your own marriage, or what it was like in your family of origin.

8. What particular pressures and satisfactions occur during the empty nest years? List some specific ones either from your own experience or the experience of someone you know well.

9. What stresses can retirement put on a marriage relationship? If you are not retired, list three specific things you can do now to reduce the pressure later on?

Chapter 10

1. In what areas do you feel you do a good job as a parent? In what areas do you feel you fall short? (If you don't have children, list some of the ways you feel your parents either did a good job or fell short.)

2. According to this chapter, how has Freudian psychology put undue pressure on parents today?

3. What are the three options we have when we fall short as Christians or as parents? Which is the most healthy?

4. What are four possible approaches to our mistakes listed in the chapter. For each, name a time in your life when you have followed that approach. What was the result? Which approach do you tend to use most?

5. List the four suggestions the authors make for making a "good enough" family work in real life.

6. List three specific strategies for nourishing your marriage relationship even amid the demands of parenting.

7. List three specific strategies for building good family memories.

8. List three tasks or chores that are always done by one person in your family. Then try to come up with at least two other ways to get that task done.

9. How do you respond to the suggestion that "spiritually, it's time to get off Dad's back"? In your family, which partner has the most interest and ability in spiritual leadership?

10. List three strategies for helping a parent's role "self-destruct" by teaching a child autonomy and independence.

Chapter 11

1. What are the three major family tasks discussed in this chapter?

2. How would you describe the "attachment style" in your family of origin? How would you describe the attachment style in your family now?

3. What are some of the "separations" you have experienced in your lifetime—both as part of your family of origin and your current family? How were these separations handled?

4. What are some of the losses that have occurred in your life? How did you respond to those losses?

5. Can you think of times in your marriage when unrecognized grief or grief masquerading as anger may have been at the root of marital conflict? If not, try to think of some other marriages you know that have been positively or negatively affected by grief and loss.

6. Which of the four families described in this chapter most closely matches your own in terms of handling attachment, separation, and loss? In what ways does your experience differ even from the one you most closely resemble?

7. As a couple, look back over your relationship thus far and trace some of the cycles of bonding and attachment, death and burial, and resurrection as far as your relationship was concerned. (You may choose to draw a kind of "time line" on a piece of paper, tracing the ups and downs of your relationship.)

8. Work together to come up with a one- or two-sentence statement of hope for your marriage. After reading this book, what are some of your expectations and promises for living together as real people in a real-life marriage?